HOW TO DESIGN AND BUILD
YOUR IDEAL
WOODSHOP

BILL STANKUS

POPULAR WOODWORKING BOOKS
CINCINNATI, OHIO

BILL STANKUS has taught woodworking at the University of Wisconsin, The University of Akron and throughout the country in seminars and wood shows. He has been studying and teaching woodworking for most of his adult life. He is an accomplished woodworker and author of Sterling's *Setting Up Your Own Woodworking Shop*. His experience gives him the unique insight required to help woodworkers with the problems and concerns of setting up a good woodworking shop.

To prevent accidents, keep safety in mind while you work. Use the safety guards installed on power equipment; they are for your protection. When working on power equipment, keep fingers away from saw blades, wear safety goggles to prevent injuries from flying wood chips and sawdust, wear headphones to protect your hearing, and consider installing a dust vacuum to reduce the amount of airborne sawdust in your woodshop. Don't wear loose clothing, such as neckties or shirts with loose sleeves, or jewelry, such as rings, necklaces or bracelets, when working on power equipment, and tie back long hair to prevent it from getting caught in your equipment.

The author and editors who compiled this book have tried to make the contents as accurate and correct as possible. Plans, illustrations, photographs and text have been carefully checked. All instructions, plans and projects should be carefully read, studied and understood before beginning construction. Due to the variability of local conditions, construction materials, skill levels, etc., neither the authors nor Popular Woodworking Books assumes any responsibility for any accidents, injuries, damages or other losses incurred resulting from the material presented in this book.

Other fine Popular Woodworking Books are available from your local bookstore or direct from the publisher.

02 01 00   5 4 3 2

Library of Congress Cataloging-in-Publication Data

Stankus, Bill.
    How to design and build your ideal woodshop / Bill Stankus.
        p.   cm.
    Includes bibliographical references and index.
    ISBN 1-55870-481-7 (pbk.: alk. paper)
    1. Workshops—Design and construction. 2. Woodwork—Equipment and supplies. 3. Woodworking tools. I. Title.
TT152.S73   1998
684'.08—dc21   98-25949
                                                                       CIP

Edited by R. Adam Blake
Content Edited by Bruce E. Stoker
Production Edited by Michelle Kramer
Interior Designed by Candace Haught
Cover Designed by Angela Lennert Wilcox

METRIC CONVERSION CHART		
TO CONVERT	TO	MULTIPLY BY
Inches	Centimeters	2.54
Centimeters	Inches	0.4
Feet	Centimeters	30.5
Centimeters	Feet	0.03
Yards	Meters	0.9
Meters	Yards	1.1
Sq. Inches	Sq. Centimeters	6.45
Sq. Centimeters	Sq. Inches	0.16
Sq. Feet	Sq. Meters	0.09
Sq. Meters	Sq. Feet	10.8
Sq. Yards	Sq. Meters	0.8
Sq. Meters	Sq. Yards	1.2
Pounds	Kilograms	0.45
Kilograms	Pounds	2.2
Ounces	Grams	28.4
Grams	Ounces	0.04

DEDICATION

This book is dedicated to my son—and assistant—Gavin Stankus

■

ACKNOWLEDGMENTS

"Woodworking" signifies many things: hobby activity, repairing an old chair, making toys, craft work, business, creating heirloom objects or simply puttering around in the workshop. However, the two key words in "woodworking" are *wood* and *working*. And, the workshop is the bridge between those two words.

This book isn't about picture-perfect workshops or catalog photographs of tools. It is an attempt to convey the message that woodworking is an active process that combines desire, experience, problem solving, materials and effort. Woodworking is truly a celebration of our need to build things.

There are a few individuals that I would like to thank for their contributions relating to this book. First Adam Blake, my editor, has been a positive and nurturing force. Writing is sometimes difficult and weird work. It's terrific to receive encouragement and support. Thanks Adam.

Alan Boardman was essential in clarifying the notion of the "ideal workshop." He once told me that as long as he had a pocketknife and could whittle, he would be content. Sometimes saying the obvious is equivalent to an encyclopedia.

I would like to thank the following woodworkers for allowing me into their workshops and for the hours we spent talking about shops, lumber, tools and woodworking enjoyment. We even solved a few of the world's problems.

Steve Balter, furniture maker

Ted Bartholomew, turner

Dean Bershaw, furniture maker

David Beyl, instructor

Charles Caswell, furniture maker

Tom Dailey, hobbyist

Robert Girdis, luthier

Steven Gray, woodwright

Hannes Hase, custom wood windows

Mark Kulseth, furniture maker

James Leary, remodeler

George Levin, furniture maker

John MacKenzie, hobbyist

Jon Magill, hobbyist

Doug Matthews, antique restoration

Curt Minier, furniture maker

CONTENTS

P. 37

P. 35

P. 37

P. 36

P. 54

P. 86

P. 16

P. 60

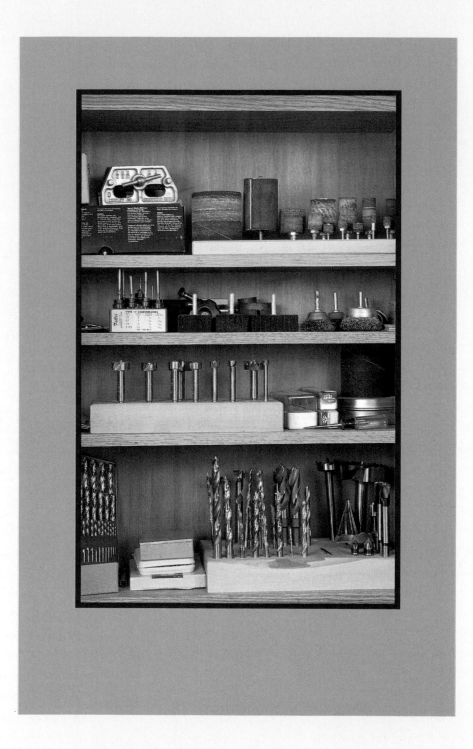

INTRODUCTION

There's an old joke about alligators and a baseball bat. Although the joke is long forgotten, the image of some poor guy surrounded by alligators and feverishly swinging the bat, trying to keep them away . . . well, it seems appropriate as an image of today's woodworker.

Twenty years ago, it was difficult to find woodworking how-to information. There were few magazines dedicated to woodworking and there weren't many woodworking tool stores or catalog houses. There certainly weren't awesome computers and Internet woodworking chat rooms. I also don't recall any PBS shows about remodeling houses, working with antique tools or building cabinets. And there wasn't a popular television comedy show about a klutzy tool user. It's amazing that we got by!

Twenty years later, we are kind of like that guy with the ball bat and the alligators. There are magazines, books, traveling woodworking sideshows, Internet sites, videotapes and TV shows discovering and revealing all of the age-old techniques and mysteries of woodworking. We have a cornucopia of tools, supplies and gizmos. And all of these things are being promoted by marketing departments attempting to get our attention. We love woodworking, but there are a lot of alligators.

Although I like routers, hand planes and scroll saws, I deliberately did not include the encyclopedia or the kitchen sink in this book. Photographs of routers and table saws age quickly. Also, it's relatively easy to call 1-800-something-or-other and receive the current edition of beautiful color product sheets or catalogs on everything from awls to zebrawood.

What I have attempted to do is answer the question, "How do I set up the ideal workshop?" The first, easy response is that the ideal workshop is *your* workshop. Throughout the book, I have presented my ideas on how to develop your workshop.

I've never liked talking about myself, but if it helps to explain my point of view, I will. I have been woodworking for over twenty years. I am self-taught—and I've enjoyed the classroom. I've worked in one of the first walk-in, fine tool stores (The Cutting Edge in Beverly Hills, California—too bad it's gone now). I've built custom furniture, carved a few things and turned a few bowls. I taught woodworking for one year at a major university (hated the bureaucracy), set up a seminar program for a tool store, and did consulting work for tool companies. I have written magazine articles, operators' manuals for the Leigh Dovetail Jig and the Multi-Router, and a bunch of video scripts on tool use that were sold at Sears. I have taught many seminars and hands-on classes throughout the country, wrote another book on setting up a woodworking shop, restored Revolutionary War-era and Gus Stickley furniture, remodeled our house and built things for my family. And another part of this crazy quilt is that this was all done in California, Wisconsin, New York and Washington.

Along the way I have met and visited with a terrific group of people—you, the American woodworkers. You and your colleagues are a great and entertaining fraternity. I honestly wish I could write all of your names in the book's dedication. The trip through the past twenty years hasn't been about money or fame—it's been about building objects, spending time in the workshop, enjoyment, doing the right thing, questing after better woodworking and, finally, sharing with each other.

Thanks everyone. Now ignore the alligators and go build something.

1

Planning Your Ideal Woodshop

The workshop will reflect your type of woodworking. Usually that means either being a generalist or a specialist.

MAKE YOUR PLANS RELEVANT

Relevance. Remember the word. Whether you are setting up a new woodshop or enhancing an existing one, it is of utmost importance to maintain a realistic goal tempered by healthy doses of relevance.

I believe there are several principles that motivate and drive the desires for a workshop. First is wanting to build something. Second is having the finances to set up the workshop. Third is having a location for the workshop. What is often missing is having some background or experience that forges and shapes

the generalizations we think are the foundations of woodworking. Unfortunately, many of us reinvent the wheel when we are attempting to design and set up a woodshop. Sometimes it's impossible to separate the wheat from the chaff when your own reference points are vague. And sometimes it's difficult to ask the right questions, simply because you haven't learned the vocabulary. Consequently, we are often making do or working with the wrong equipment in an inappropriate space.

Many of us set up workshops without a reference point, such as that provided by a trade school or a master craftsman. The advantage of not having had years of training from a master craftsman is being free to pick and choose everything from

adzes to zebrawood—and using them for whatever seems appropriate. The disadvantage is that we don't have someone's hard-earned experiences to guide us. Being self-taught, we can't call upon traditions to specify project design or answer questions such as, "Should I buy a table saw or a band saw first?" And therein is the crux of the problem. How does one design and organize a workshop? It's a tough question that, when answered, can lead one through the full spectrum from happiness to misery.

If you are fortunate, you will have friends with useful woodshop experiences, and you will have ideas about what you want to do in a woodshop. Most areas have clubs or guilds that are great resource centers because their main purpose is advancing woodworking knowledge. Their members are motivated by an interest in woodworking and a desire to socialize with other woodworkers. While there are clubs that focus on general woodworking, there are also specialized clubs for carving, turning, model making and other unique endeavors. Visit these clubs both for problem-solving information and for camaraderie.

FINDING THE PERFECT WOODSHOP

The thorny topic of master woodworkers as sources of information must be addressed. There is no question that a skilled craftsman can inspire, motivate and educate. I can think of no better person to go to for learning about cutting dovetail joints, applying lacquer, carving or turning. These individuals have spent a lifetime learning the skills that most of us cherish. However, some caution is in order when looking at their workshops. I would suggest that the workshop of a seasoned craftsman or master woodworker is akin to a comfortable, but worn, pair of leather shoes, which fit only one person. Anyone else who tries to wear those shoes will get pinched toes, sore ankles or fallen arches. So, too, is the workshop of the craftsman: The shop is an extension of the person. The layout, the equipment and the open

space all reflect personal interests, habits and projects. Additionally, the temperament, rationalizations and judgments of a craftsman are imperfect. Even the masters have learned from a limited sampling of woodworking experiences. A person taught to use computer-controlled machines in a German trade school probably hasn't experienced the portability of a traditional Japanese craftsman's tool chest. Nor is the proponent of wooden planes necessarily interested in using an air nailer.

Setting aside the meticulousness of engineers and patternmakers, I don't know of any woodworker who approaches woodshop organization using the scientific method. Nor do I know of anyone using a consumer's research system or product review method to identify woodshop organization in a precise and controlled way. Instead, we organize in a facile and casual manner and let our pocketbook and free time steer us into tools, storage and gizmos. However, because we are spending our hard-earned time and money, we should try to be somewhat methodical and logical when organizing the woodshop. Ignorance might be blissful, but it's not the best approach when organizing the woodshop.

The old expression "jack of all trades and master of none" does

indeed apply to workshop organization. Typically, the novice woodworker thinks that there is a particular set of tools and equipment that should be in any workshop. The scenario develops something like, "I need a table saw, band saw, jointer, planer, drill press, router table or shaper, dust collector, air compressor, disc and belt sanders, workbench, tool chests, all portable power tools (including three routers) and every clamp known to mankind." "After all," you say to yourself, "there must be a reason for a hundred different router jigs and templates being in the marketplace. And don't the toolmakers and sellers know more about all of this than I do?" My advice is to show restraint and buy tools and equipment with caution and prudence. In fact, if you want to include a tool in your workshop because it was used on a TV woodworking show or demonstrated at a woodworking seminar, be wary; that tool might have been shown simply as a sales and marketing ploy.

The media has also fostered the notion that there is a "perfect" workshop complete with stationary and portable tools, uncluttered storage and room left over for the car, water skis and a winter's worth of firewood. There are so many references to the ideal positioning of equipment and workbenches, and the logical flow of work from machine to machine, that it seems the goal is to have an efficient production business instead of a neat and useful woodshop. I have never seen a workshop plan that matches my workshop with regard to type of machines, size of the workbench, available wall storage or family cooperation about not parking their bicycles in the shop. However, we do need to begin the planning and organization of the workshop with some type of personal perspective; otherwise, the workshop might end up looking like a hardware store. There should be a reference back to the three guiding principles: woodworking inclination, money and space. Ask yourself these questions: "What do I want to build? What do I want to spend? Where will I do the work?"

TYPICAL WORKSHOPS

Some of the basic requirements for a workshop are sufficient room size, machines, hand and power tools, workbench, lumber storage, tool storage, assembly area, dust collection, air circulation and ventilation and proper lighting. Each of these requirements has some application to all woodworking endeavors. How these requirements apply are a function of your woodworking interest. Tool storage, for example, is different for carvers and turners. And side lighting, although

useful for carvers, isn't generally useful when making cabinets.

The Furniture or Cabinetry Workshop

If there is such a thing as a general-purpose workshop, the furniture or cabinetry workshop might be it. Here is where we find the most general-purpose machines, tools and accessories. Why? Because furnituremaking and cabinetmaking require basic cuts and joinery that are thought to be the domain of the basic power tool group (whatever that is). It's worth noting that tool and machine manufacturers rarely state that their products are designed for specific constructions. Their product information emphasizes the general nature—or usefulness, accuracy or precision—of nonspecific functions. That is because companies deliberately design these products for general use. The exceptions to this are tools designed for a specific function, such as biscuit joinery machines or dovetail jigs. Generally, someone who has been building furniture or cabinets for years has a repetitive woodworking style and probably has a basic collection of tools to match that repetition. For example, I like to make table legs that have 1″×2″ round tenons that fit 1″ diameter through-mortises in the table top. To simplify cutting the round tenons, I made a jig out

of plywood to use with a router. The setup is fast and easy, and it takes very little time to make a set of legs. Consequently, I find it natural to design furniture using the round-tenon jig, so I use it frequently. Thus, the workshop becomes simplified through the process of repetition.

ROOM SIZE Furniture building and cabinetwork require a room that permits the safe operation of machines and other tools. There should be *safe zones* around machines such as table saws, so that the operator and anyone else in the woodshop can stand in an uncluttered and safe location while the machine is running. It is also necessary to allow enough space to move any workpiece to and from a machine without being obstructed. Yellow or orange safety tape stuck to the floor can be used to define this safety zone.

The furniture and cabinetry shop should be large enough to accommodate typical machines, a workbench, storage cabinets and lumber storage. Mobile bases can be attached to machines so they can be stored out of the way when not in use, but remember, even mobile machines require floor area for storage. Although a machine can be moved to create an open area, it still has to be stored somewhere.

Consider this point when arranging the work area.

An assembly area, or open space, is necessary for putting things together. Think of open space as an object, similar to a woodbench or table saw. When designing your woodshop, be certain to include enough room for assembling the largest piece of furniture to be built. Factor in the following: moving workpieces for assembly; access to, and positioning of, bar clamps; flat and even flooring; and whether the workpiece can be left in this location while other tools or machines are used. Ideally, this open space should be away from stationary machines and near the workbench and clamp storage. And if the workpiece will have finishes applied at this location, the space should be away from any heat sources (e.g., water heaters, furnaces or sparking motors) to avoid fire danger.

LUMBER STORAGE Lumber storage is typically very low-tech in the furniture workshop. The most common storage technique is to pile it on the floor or lean it against a wall. Lumber is heavy, and for safety reasons shouldn't be stored at too great a height. If wall racks are used, take care to build the racks sturdy and strong. There are several commercial wall racks suited for lumber storage. However, suitable storage can be made from 2 × 4s at a fraction of the cost. A simple storage rack need be nothing more than an open frame structure. If you need to store short lengths, the structure can be shelved in with plywood or particleboard. Another simple lumber storage system consists of 2 × 4s or 4 × 4s, vertically bolted to wall studs, with sturdy dowels or metal rods inserted into holes. The dowels should project no more than five inches from the post. Don't place heavy clamps at the ends of the dowels—keep the heavier ones near the post.

A very real option for the hobby woodworker is to let the lumberyard store the wood. Purchase what you need prior to starting a project. If the environment of your woodshop is significantly wetter, drier, hotter or colder than the lumberyard, purchase the lumber a month or so before you plan to start construction to allow the wood to acclimate to the workshop. Small pieces of wood (good scrap pieces and cutoff pieces) usually are stored in boxes and bins and on shelves. I believe there is a Murphy's Law concerning these pieces: "If they are left alone in a box on a shelf, their numbers will multiply and they will never go away!" Some woodworkers actually burn scrap wood in woodburning stoves.

MACHINERY Never before in the history of the world has there been such a variety of woodworking tools. It would take several football stadiums to display one of each machine model from all of the world's manufacturers. Today's woodworker can own an infinite combination of machines for making furniture. Selecting the machines that best satisfy your requirements is time-consuming and difficult. Most experts suggest the basic furniture-making machines: table saw, radial-arm saw, band saw, lathe, shaper/router table, drill press, jointer and planer. While this a predictable (and expensive) answer, there are other approaches for determining the machinery you need.

Keep in mind what you are planning to build, and avoid the notion that a general-purpose tool might be useful at a later date. Create a budget for machinery and set high and low dollar amounts. Next, visit with friends and acquaintances who enjoy woodworking. Ask questions about favorite machines, warranties, accuracy, maintenance, durability, accessories, spare parts and other concerns of this sort. Obtain specification and price sheets from manufacturers. Use caution when visiting retail stores selling machinery. Using the table saw as an example, no store is large enough to display all of the models from one manufacturer, let alone all of the table saws from all of the manufacturers. Most retail stores are going to attempt to sell you whatever is in stock—but the saw that they *don't* sell may be the perfect one for your needs.

Once you have a list of potential machinery, add up the costs and look at your budget. But don't get discouraged and go out and buy a new truck instead. If the cost exceeds your budget, ask yourself, "Do I need that machine? Is there an alternate way to do the work? Can I use machines at the local school? What about combination machines? Hand tools?"

If you are a beginning furniture maker or cabinetmaker, start with good-quality and reasonably priced machines such as a contractor's 10" table saw, a 14" bandsaw, a 6" or a 8" jointer and a portable 12" planer. Look for sale prices or buy used (but not worn-out) machines. Work with these machines for a while until you understand their functions and foibles and how they apply to your own work. In time, as your skills improve, you can sell them (there's always a market for used machines) and move up to better or more specialized machines. If you have a limited budget, selling your older machine to buy a newer one is a great way to afford better tools.

Take your time when buying machines. There is nothing wrong with having a five- or ten-year plan. That is, use your machines, complement them with hand tools and plan for future purchases based upon your current woodworking interests. Perhaps a mortising machine—or dovetail jig or wide-belt sander—might suit your needs once you have spent time making furniture without them. Doing without is a wonderful woodworking process, because it allows you to solve problems and appreciate the real value of a woodworking machine.

HAND TOOLS AND POWER TOOLS Selecting hand tools and power tools requires the same process as that for machinery. The appealing nature and cost of these tools make them easier to purchase and store. The problem is that, after reading a typical tool catalog, it seems that every tool is necessary for the woodshop. The reasonable thing to do is look at the construction process for your work and then decide whether a monster miter saw or battery-powered router is really necessary. The new home improvement centers (the modern version of hardware stores) are great for browsing and handling tools. It's important to touch hand tools, to experience their heft, balance and physical nature. But

remember, don't buy a tool unless you need it—and need it for more than one project.

WORKBENCH Furniture makers and cabinetmakers require a workbench. Size, shape and number of vises are matters of personal taste. I know of woodworkers who use their bench as a catch-all surface, and others who treat the workbench as a piece of fine furniture. The workbench is usually positioned against a wall or located so that it can be accessed from all four sides. The workbench should have the flattest reference surface in the workshop so that it can also be used as a clamping surface. In my opinion, a traditional workbench is OK for building furniture with traditional hand tools, but if you are using routers, portable belt sanders and other modern tools, the workbench should be designed with those tools in mind.

TOOL STORAGE Furniture and cabinetry shops probably have the greatest array of tools, accessories, jigs and fixtures of any woodshop because this type of woodworking requires assorted layout and measuring tools, chisels, saws, sharpening equipment, mallets, hammers and accessories for all the power tools. Generally, these items are stored in chests or drawers, or are hung on walls.

Some potential furnituremakers and cabinetmakers get distracted from their goal of making furniture and instead pursue the notion of the "perfect" workshop: Drawers and cabinets are designed to store (or showcase) pristine tool collections. While there is nothing wrong with collecting, *functional* storage should be the goal if you plan to use the tools.

DUST COLLECTION Until recently, woodshops with piles of sawdust mounded around table saws and jointers were the norm: Heaps of chips were a sign that something was being made in the workshop. Thankfully, times have changed. Furniture and cabinet shops can now be reasonably free of chips and dust, because numerous types of dust collection units designed to fit any size of workshop are available. The portable units take about the same amount of floor space as a band saw; built-in units can be as large as you want or need. Most dust collectors are affordable, so there is no reason to have potentially dangerous and unhealthy dust in the workshop.

AIR CIRCULATION AND VENTILATION
Workshops need adequate air circulation. Windows, fans, open doors or any other system of venting the room to provide fresh air is a must. If the workshop is located in a basement, humidity and lack of fresh air can rust tools and cause finishing products to set up poorly. And as the basement environment cycles between dry during the winter, when the furnace is operating, and the warm humidity of summer, wood that is stored there will react accordingly. For example, drawers that work smoothly in the winter may swell with the summer's humidity and not open.

One air-quality problem that is unique to basement workshops is radon radiation not dissipating due to poor air circulation. Radon is most commonly found when basements are located over shale, and the radiation seeps upward and into the workshop through cracked basement walls and floors. Patching these cracks is a good idea.

Fumes from finishing products and solvents, when confined to a closed room, are another potential hazard. Furthermore, many finishing products that evaporate into the air are flammable either as a li quid or as a vapor. Using flammable products in a closed room with a furnace, water heater or other heat source near by is a good way to end up with TV coverage of firemen hosing down the rubble of what was once your woodshop.

LIGHTING Mood lighting doesn't help make furniture and cabinets. The ideal lighting should be glare-free, shadow-free, color-balanced and visually comfortable. If it were possible, I would like my workshop to have every light source possible: windows, a skylight, and incandescent and fluorescent lights. If windows and skylights aren't possible, the best artificial lighting is a combination of incandescent and daylight-balanced fluorescent lights. The fluorescent lights cover the overall workshop, and incandescent lights enhance specific work areas (e.g., above the workbench and at machines).

The Carver's Workshop

ROOM SIZE Woodcarvers are very fortunate when it comes to choosing work areas, as the possibilities are almost unlimited. Carving tools can be packed up in a shoe box and taken to a vacation locale, so a seat under a palm tree becomes the work shop. Or woodcarvers can have beautiful, state-of-the art workshops with room to carve old-fashioned circus wagons. But most woodcarvers work in modest-size shops in garages, spare bedrooms or a basement corner. Compact work areas (50 to 100 square feet) are common.

MACHINES The diversity of wood-carving makes it difficult to generalize about the typical machines used. With that said, a modest-size band saw, scroll saw, drill press and motorized grinding wheel (for sharpening) are the most commonly found machines. Woodcarvers do more rough shaping of wood than the precise type of cutting found in a cabinet shop. Also, carvers can work on thicker or smaller workpieces than are found in a furniture shop. If power rotary carving tools are to be used frequently, a small dust collector or shop vacuum should be included in the workshop.

HAND TOOLS AND POWER TOOLS Woodcarving tools are generally either traditional chisels and mallets or power rotary tools. And rarely does a woodcarver use only one carving chisel. Generally, chisels are grouped as a complementary set (10mm #5 straight, 20mm #31 spoon bit, 12mm V-tool and so forth). Chisels are also long, short, stubby and microsize. Some are meant to be hand pushed; others are to be hit with a mallet. Rotary tools require AC, battery or air power. And there are hundreds of carving burrs and abrasive points from which to choose. What this means is that the carver's shop requires thoughtful storage for easy access to potentially hun-

dreds of tools that vary in size from 1" to 18". Furthermore, there are mallets, sharpening tools, drill bits and assorted knives to use and store.

WORKBENCH One key requirement of a woodcarver's bench is that it must be capable of holding a workpiece rigid. When carving a statue, the workpiece is typically held vertically, and carving is done 360° around the piece. As work progresses, the workpiece needs to be moved so that work proceeds evenly around it. To do this, the workpiece must constantly be clamped, unclamped, repositioned and reclamped. Typical front and end vises are not designed for this type of holding. However, specially designed workpiece holders that mount directly to the workbench and can be rotated 360° are available for carvers.

Typically, woodcarvers use smaller benches those that of cabinetmakers. Some workbenches are about the same size as a bar stool. If using a mallet and chisels, the workbench must be heavy enough to absorb the constant vibrations from the mallet blows. Power carving also requires working 360° around the workpiece, but since it doesn't produce heavy mallet hits, the workbench doesn't have to be as stout.

For smaller carving projects

(that is, the bird-in-the-hand size), the workbench probably will be used as a place to rest tools while working. A TV tray is actually adequate for small carving work. If you are sitting down, it's large enough to hold a few tools and catch the workpiece chips.

For carvers, the workbench is the assembly area. Carved workpieces are not usually the size of furniture, so a separate area is not required.

WOOD STORAGE I haven't seen many woodcarver's workshops that have racks of long lumber. Instead, woodcarvers tend to have boxes and bins of small wood pieces: cutoff pieces, firewood-size chunks, limbs and slabs of wood. Generally, the reasons for racking lumber (flatness, moisture control, etc.) aren't as necessary for woodcarving. Shelves and bins are perfectly acceptable for storing woodcarving wood.

TOOL STORAGE The woodcarvers I have known all have had a similar work environment in one respect: Their work area is like that of a piano player; that is, most of their tools are within easy reach when sitting or standing at the workbench. Consequently, tool chests with plenty of small drawers, tool racks behind the workbench or even coffee cans filled with tools sitting on the workbench are common types of storage. Power carving tools are generally suspended over the workbench or hung on nails next to the bench, and the grinder for sharpening is equally close at hand.

DUST COLLECTION It's difficult to remove wood chips while carving. The old expression "let the chips fall where they may" still applies. The great thing about using a mallet, chisels and knives is that the chips do fall to the floor and you aren't breathing dust. However, when using power tools, the dust flies through the air and into faces and lungs. It's not uncommon to watch a power carver, using a rotary tool, doing detail work fairly close to his face. Obviously, safety goggles and dust masks should be used, but the addition of a dust collector for drawing the dust away from the work area would be ideal.

AIR CIRCULATION AND VENTILATION Several conditions make air circulation and ventilation very important. Paints and other finishing products should be used in a well-ventilated area. Again, many finishing products are potential fire hazards. But even if the finishing products are not flammable, it is best to vent the room so that you (and others) don't have to breathe the chemical fumes. Carvers also enjoy work-

ing with unusual and exotic woods, like apple wood or cocobolo. Some woods can cause skin irritation, so efforts should be made to work as cleanly as possible.

LIGHTING Since most carving workshops are in small areas, fewer lighting fixtures are needed than in a cabinet shop. Ideally, the carver's shop should have both incandescent and fluorescent overhead lighting with separate on/off switches. Side light is very useful for the carver. By turning off the overhead lights and using side lighting from a table-top goose-neck lamp or other type of lamp, the workpiece will have different shadows, which helps to visually reveal textures.

The Lathe Turner's Workshop

Wood turning is aptly named, because every time you turn around there are new lathe and tool innovations and new lathe techniques. The past fifteen years have seen incredible developments in wood turning: new lathe designs for turning bowls, spindles and miniatures; new shapes in turning tools and an armada of workpiece holding devices; and, to make it even better, a new generation of wood turning instructors, instructional videos, magazines and wood-turner's clubs as sources of information.

ROOM SIZE The basic lathe turner's workshop can be compact, with enough room for the lathe, other tools, machines and storage. The basic nature of wood turning allows the work project to be started and finished on the lathe, which means there is little need for additional room space for other types of wood processing. Because the lathe is usually located against a wall, with the operator in a more or less static position, the wood turner can easily set up the woodshop in a garage or basement.

MACHINES The traditional wood lathe has undergone considerable design changes because of the heightened interest in bowl turning. In the old days, lathes had long beds with 36" to 48" distances between centers and were mostly used for turning stair spindles and other long pieces. These lathes generally had a 6" distance from centers to bed surface, which meant that a 12" bowl was the maximum capacity over the bed. Bowls of greater size were meant to be turned "outboard," on the opposite side of the head stock, if the lathe had that capacity. Today's turners often use both the head and tail stock for support while turning bowls. That means the distance from centers to bed should be adequate to turn larger diameter bowls. Many lathes now have

Hobbyist John MacKenzie has under-floor dust collection ductwork.

this capacity and other useful features, such as DC motors, which permit variable turning speeds starting at zero RPM (AC motor variable speeds usually begin at about 500 RPM), as well.

Other machines common to wood turner's workshops are band saws, dust collectors and grinders. Table saws, jointers and planers can be useful for wood preparation, but they aren't a necessity.

HAND TOOLS AND POWER TOOLS There are many tools and accessories that aid in wood turning. A few of the more important power tools are a cordless drill for attaching face plates, a finish sander for sanding the workpiece while it's still mounted on the lathe, a rotary tool for detail work and sanding, and a jigsaw or saber saw

for preliminary shaping. There are many useful measuring devices, such as inside and outside calipers and center finders. If hand tools are used, it's probably for preliminary wood removal or for unique detail design work.

WORKBENCH In a sense, the lathe *is* the workbench. Once the preliminary shaping of the workpiece is done, just about everything else is done at the lathe. The other ongoing activity while turning is sharpening; for convenience, most turners install a grinder next to the lathe. A small workbench or counter top is useful for the odds and ends of setup or take-down work. Aside from those activities, the workbench is used for sorting wood and other miscellaneous tasks.

LUMBER STORAGE Depending upon your zealousness, storing wood can range from a few pieces to filling the garage, deck and barns with chunks of wood. If you are collecting wood and searching for downed trees in orchards, yards, parks and forests, you will need adequate storage. Not only will you need room to store the freshly cut (often referred to as *green* or *wet*) wood, but you will also need storage areas for the drier pieces. To further complicate the picture, there should be a functional inventory system so that different species can be identified—without leaves, one chunk of wood is difficult to tell from another.

TOOL STORAGE Lathe turning, billiards and golf have one thing in common: They all require easy access to long, thin tools. Neat and tidy storage for lathe tools is indeed similar to racks designed to hold cues. But don't make a rack for 12 tools and then buy 13. One possiblity is to make a wall rack that can accommodate a growing tool collection. Another easy solution is pegboard-covered walls near the lathe. A roll-around cart also permits easy access to lathe tools, and it's less limited in the number of tools it can hold.

ASSEMBLY AREA The assembly or construction area is at the lathe itself. Off lathe work consists of activities such as tool sharpening, wood preparation and detailing and finishing work.

DUST COLLECTION Depending on whether wet or dry wood is turned, the debris will come off the turning as long stringy pieces or as smaller bits and dust. A good dust collection system will not only make the lathe work neater and easier, but also keep the debris from traveling many feet away from the lathe. Without dust collection, the debris field (especially that of green or wet wood) looks like a confetti celebration—of carrot peelings. Ideally, a dust collection port should be positioned behind and near the turning area. Articulated ductwork with a port is especially useful when it can be repositioned for any work angle or location.

AIR CIRCULATION AND VENTILATION
Moving dust and chips away from the work area also means cleaner air for the lathe operator. A simple solution is to position an electric fan near the work, so that it moves air (and dust) away from the operator, preferably toward a window or door.

Many turners use helmets with face guards that have built-in fans and filters. These battery-powered units filter air at the back of the helmet and move clean air across the face area.

LIGHTING Pleasant overhead lighting is a necessity in the wood turner's shop. It's advantageous to be able to turn different lights on and off so that wood surface textures and features can be easily viewed from different lighting angles. Isolated spotlights aimed at the work area are also useful for watching how cutting tools perform against wood.

The Furniture Restorer's Workshop

Furniture restoration and repair workshops have to be more versatile than the typical furniture making, lathe turning or carving shops. That's because the restorer has to be able to set up the workshop so that almost every woodworking skill can be performed. For example, replacement chair rungs must be turned on a lathe, broken decorations must be carved, and drawer sides and bottoms must be cut to a specific size and thickness. Even if you specialize in one particular item (chairs), it's difficult to know what demands the next broken piece will make on the woodshop.

ROOM SIZE Restoring jewelry boxes, dining room sets, antique hall mirrors or a drop-front desk obviously creates very different room requirements.

The workshop has to have enough room for three functions: storage of broken pieces, space

to fabricate replacement pieces using tools and machines in a workshop filled with workpieces and, finally, space for cleaning, disassembly, gluing-up and reassembly. I spent many years restoring turn-of-the-century Arts and Crafts (Mission style) furniture, and the sizes of those pieces were always a problem. Sideboards and settles (benches) are large, heavy and difficult to move. If several pieces were brought into my workshop, suddenly the room got smaller. So plan enough space to store works-in-progress as well as the machines to work on them.

MACHINES Unlike furniture and cabinet shops, where machines are required for a significant portion of the construction process, the same machines are minimally used for restoration. The chair or table is already made; it just needs a part or two. The emphasis thus shifts to the need for high-quality machines to make occasional replacement parts. If I could assign a proportional value to the need for machines in restoration work, I would say that need is less significanct than other factors. Far more important is understanding how to use various joinery techniques, using chemicals or gluing-up odd-shaped pieces.

You may use a lathe to make bowls (for your own enjoyment),

View of Doug Matthews' workshop. The sliding glass doors are often left open in good weather.

but very rarely do you need a lathe to restore bowls. Instead, the restorer's lathe will be used to turn replacement spindles, posts and rungs, so its main feature should be bed length (distance between centers).

A high-quality saw blade is the most important feature of a table saw for restoration work, because it's often necesssary to make tear-out-free and odd-angle cuts through antique wood. The aim is to waste as little as possible of the irreplaceable original

wood. Band saws should have ⅛″ or ¼″ smooth cutting blades so that clean radius cuts can be made easily.

The same kind of careful evaluation should be applied to other machines as well. For example, a planer with a slow feed rate is preferred for planing highly figured wood.

HAND TOOLS AND POWER TOOLS I firmly believe that successful restoration work requires the use of an array of traditional hand tools and

power tools. For example, a desk or cabinet from the early 1800s probably was built with hand-cut dovetails. If the piece has boards that are damaged beyond repair, replacement wood will need hand-cut dovetails made to match the original. That means using a tenon saw, chisels, a marking gauge and a mallet. Or there may be hardened glue in a dowel hole that resists being picked out. Using a rotary tool with a round burr might be the only method of removing the dried glue.

The tool selection for restoration work is eclectic due to the variety of potential repairs. Bench planes, moulding planes, routers with specialty cutters, scrapers, chisels, wire brushes, screw extractors, band clamps and putty knives are but a few of the tools that make work easier.

WORKBENCH The traditional workbench with front and shoulder vises is useful to the restorer simply because that prized antique now being restored was originally built at such a bench. And duplicating the original construction process will lead to a better and more valuable restoration. However, if you have the room, a low workbench (approximately 12″ to 24″ high) is also very useful. A 4′×8′ sheet of ¾″ particle board laminated with melamine and resting on low sawhorses is ideal for general cleaning and disassembly. Melamine cleans easily, resists most glues and can be turned over for another clean side if it becomes scratched.

LUMBER STORAGE Just what is the lumber in a restoration workshop? I like to have bins of wood pieces sorted by color—dark, light, reds and tans—so that colors can be quickly matched with the workpiece. And I have storage for pieces from discarded furniture and other devices. I once had to replace a spindle in a

Windsor chair that dated to approximately 1795. I searched for months to find a piece of ash that had a similar color and grain pattern. My search ended when I found an old garden rake handle that was a perfect match. Now I save all sorts of wood simply because I never know when it will be useful. I also like to keep veneer pieces stored between plywood covers, an arrangement resembling a scrapbook. Full rolls of veneer should be kept rolled and wrapped in paper to keep them clean and out of the workshop air.

FINISHING PRODUCTS AND STORAGE
Don't be casual about storing finishing materials, finishing products and solvents. Specialized metal cabinets for storing hazardous and flammable materials are available, and there are specialized trash cans for oily rags and other flammable waste products. Check in the yellow pages under "safety equipment" for a source for storage cabinets. Also, all finishing materials and products should be stored a safe distance away from any heat source or direct, all-day exposure to sunlight. Finally, keep all finishing supplies away from those who aren't trained in their usage.

AIR CIRCULATION AND VENTILATION If you have done any paint stripping or furniture repair, the words

methylene chloride should speak volumes to you. *Lacquer thinner, paint thinner, benzene, MEK, alcohol, turpentine* and *wood bleach* should also be words that warn of dangerous products that require careful use. Since the earliest days of the industrial revolution, chemicals have been both a blessing and disaster to man. The phrase "mad as a hatter" referred to those who made hats with poisonous chemicals. The first photographers worked with their faces directly over mercury-coated glass plates while developing film plates. These photographers didn't have long lives; old-time restorers who worked for long periods breathing formaldehyde and other toxic chemicals didn't live long either. If having a long and healthy life is important to you, avoid chemical risks and work with intelligence and caution. Know the chemicals that you are using and follow all product safety notices. Store and use all finishing products as if they were the most dangerous liquids in the house. (They probably are.) Think of your skin and clothes as if they were sponges, eager to absorb any oil, solvent, bleach, dye or stain. Build and set up the workshop with whatever it takes to be safe.

LIGHTING Restoration work should be done with proper lighting. Ideally, the lighting should be color balanced to simulate the room in which the repaired piece will eventually reside. It's worth asking the question about the room light before starting on any repair or restoration projects. Since there's a variety of different color-balanced fluorescent lights, keep a supply of these available. The lighting tubes can then be replaced according to need.

Restoration work also benefits from side lighting. That is, a strong light source angled from a horizontal location will cast shadows on the work area. These shadows will enhance wood grain, carved surfaces, etc. and make detailing work easier.

2

CHOOSING THE RIGHT SHOP LOCATION

■

The ideal woodshop location is the location that you have; just enhance it. If I could cross my fingers and make a wish, like most woodworkers I would wish for a separate building for a workshop. It would have 1500 square feet, high ceilings, skylights, one or two windows with views of rivers and mountains, an oversize door (maybe even a garage door), wood flooring, 110V and 220V electrical supplies, plumbing with sinks and a toilet, sound-insulated walls and a smaller secondary room just for displaying the things I've made.

Setting idealism aside, I know that I have a workshop, a place where I can do woodworking. And that is perhaps the most important reality. In fact, this realization should always be the main consideration in the quest

This is the view from my workshop window. In the distance, beyond the trees, are the Olympic Mountains. The little house is for a water well.

Steve Balter has a display room in the front of his workshop.

for the ideal workshop. If you have a space that is usable, which is more important, the workshop or the things that you make? It's easy to be distracted by pinup pictures of fancy or well-appointed workshops. What is more difficult to see in the coffee-table workshop book pictures is that the ideal workshop is really nothing more than the workshop that is your own, where you can happily practice your woodworking. You can always improve on fixtures, storage and so on, but those things can evolve as you do your woodworking.

Most of us use the garage or basement for our woodshops. Sometimes, if we are doing less messy work, we might be able to use a second bedroom or part of the laundry room, but the rooms with the most space for a shop

are garages and basements. However, organizing a garage or basement is not necessarily a simple task. Garages are storage tunnels and basements are storage holes. Room proportions and construction materials differ, and using either room means displacing specific home utility functions.

THE GARAGE

Typically, garages are for one or two cars; this translates into approximately 10' × 20' (200 square feet) for one car and about 20' × 20' (400 square feet) for two cars. Garages usually have a garage door, a door into the house and a window. They can also have wall-mounted cabinets, a water heater, a built-in vacuum system for the house, a laundry and overhead storage (an attic or open rafters). Garages in newer houses are generally framed, but can also be constructed of concrete blocks or brick.

Let me create a hypothetical garage for the sake of solving a space-utilization problem and designing a workshop. Imagine a two-car garage in which the car is actually parked at night. In addition, the garage is used to store bicycles, sports equipment and garden tools. It has one window on a side wall, a door into the house and a door to the outside. Other noteworthy features include open rafters, one 4' × 5'

wall-hung cabinet, the house electrical service panel, one overhead light and AC outlets on three walls.

Because the car is destined to remain in the garage for a certain number of hours each day, only the walls and the overhead areas can be used for permanent storage. These storage areas will determine the actual design and composition of the workshop. Remember, even though the car will be outside when machines are placed in the open central area, the equipment all has to be returned to the wall areas or ceiling when the car is parked inside.

Begin by making a list of all permanent storage: household items, sports equipment and so on. Next, make a list of woodworking machines, tools and supplies that you own, and also a list of things you plan to acquire. Now, using ¼" graph paper, draw a floor plan of the garage, including doors, windows and steps (use ¼" = 1'). On a separate sheet of graph paper, using the same scale, draw all machines, cabinets and storage containers that you want in the workshop. Cut these drawings out.

Obviously, there is less area available than the floor area required when the car is inside. Judicious wall and overhead storage is necessary to open up the workshop area. So begin by re-

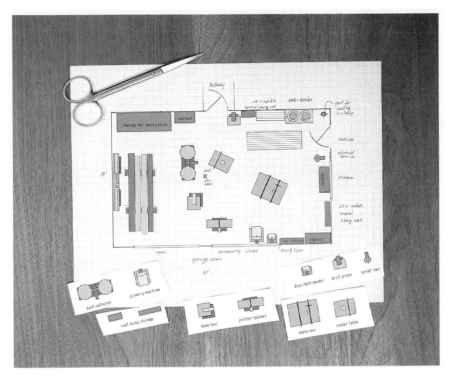

Use the icons on page 24 and lay out your shop on ¼" graph paper.

Item	Dimensions	Area (in sq. ft.)
car	6′×15′	90
household storage	2′×5′	10
sports equipment	2′×6′	12
garden tools	1′×4′	4
tool cabinet no. 1	2′×4′	8
tool cabinet no. 2	2′×5′	10
workbench	3′×6′	18
table saw	4′×4′	16
band saw	3′×3′	9
drill press	2′×2′	4
jointer	1′×4′	4
planer	2′×2′	4
dust collector	2′×3′	6
lumber storage	2′×8′	16
Total area required		211
Garage	10′×20′	200

best approach might be to develop an overall plan that unifies the entire room using a design that incorporates both house and woodshop items. This plan might include floor-to-ceiling storage units near the garage door consisting of broom-type cabinets for storing rakes and shovels, with compartments for flower pots, located beside cabinets for storing skis and tennis rackets, with drawers for storing camping supplies. Similar built-in units could be used for tools and supplies. Specialized features would allow for a lumber rack, a workbench and a clamp rack. Add mobile bases to your machines so they can be stored against the walls and easily moved to the center area when the car is parked outside. This unified design might even create enough open space so that some work (not machine work) can be done at the workbench even when the car is inside. Once there is a workable layout, the details of flooring, wall insulation, electrical service, lighting, ventilation and security can be addressed.

thinking the common ideas of storage. Consider ripping out the garage cabinet furnished by the house builders. Don't anticipate using secondhand bookcases, old kitchen cabinets, inexpensive metal shelvings or any other combination of odds and ends, and resist the urge to build new cabinets and storage units until you are reasonably certain of your needs and requirements. Sacrifice all of these things in the name of efficiency. In fact, the

Flooring

If the garage floor is cracked, rough or oil-stained, it should be cleaned, repaired or reconditioned before any other remodeling. Cracked or rough concrete floors make it difficult to move

Jon Magill converted his garage into a workshop, and two of the car bays are used for woodworking. When the cars are parked outside, mobile machines and portable workstations are moved into their locations. There is ample open area for most construction projects.

This workshop is permanently set up in a garage. Note the skylights, indirect lights, air filtration box and the location of workbench relative to the permanent wall storage/countertop area.

machines and construction projects. Casters are generally too small to roll over wide cracks, and mobile bases may not work well on rough or uneven floors. Engine-oil stains, besides being ugly, will contaminate wood and shoes.

There are several options for restoring, repairing or resurfacing concrete floors.

1. Remove oil and grease stains with liquid degreaser, or have the floor steam cleaned.
2. Use concrete patching compounds to patch chips, holes and cracks. Cracks should be thoroughly cleaned and then filled with concrete repair caulk or patching compound.
3. If the floor is too rough, consult with a floor finishing com-

pany that specializes in applying smooth surface coats.
4. Consider alternative flooring materials: floor paint, rubberized tile or linoleum-type material.

Insulating Walls

Insulating a garage makes it more energy efficient and helps moderate ambient temperature. Insulation also acts as a sound barrier and reduces machine noise, both to the inside of the house or externally to the neighbor's house.

If the garage is already finished with wallboard, you will have to make a remodeling decision. One choice would be to remove the wallboard, install insulation between the studs and

replace the wallboard. Alternatives to this approach include:

1. Hiring an insulating company to drill holes in the wall and blow insulation into the wall cavities.
2. Attaching solid or rigid insulation board (sometimes referred to as *blueboard*) with a vapor barrier directly to the existing wallboard and then covering it with new wallboard. **Note:** This extends the walls outward about 1 ½".
3. Covering the existing walls with plywood or pegboard and painting them with fire-retardant paint.
4. Weatherstripping both interior and exterior doors.
5. Insulating the garage door. Be aware that this is not as easy as insulating walls. If the

garage door is solid construction, solid insulation board could be attached to it. But don't make the door too heavy. Check with garage door companies regarding appropriate door weight and other methods of insulation. All insulation types are rated with numbers called *R-values*, which have been established by the U.S. Department of Energy for walls, floors and ceilings in different climate zones in the United States. Some manufacturers of insulation recommend R-values higher than the Department of Energy's recommendations. These higher R-value recommendations are usually based on the concept that more insulation is more energy efficient. Obviously, workshops in Santa Monica, California, require less insulation than workshops in Milwaukee, Wisconsin. Check with your local insulation suppliers to determine the correct R-values for your specific climate zone.

If you don't want machine sounds blasting through the garage door, drape sound insulation (and fireproof) curtains in front of the garage door. Or use manufactured garage doors made with insulation materials.

Electrical Service and Wiring

Not having adequate electrical power in a woodshop is like having a sports car without gasoline.

No matter how fine the woodworking machines are or how sophisticated the lighting, unless the electrical service is specifically designed for the workshop, you may as well whittle with a pocketknife. Not only do machines require adequate power for operation, but it is unsafe to use any electrical tool with an inadequate power supply, and underpowered electrical tools will wear out faster, as well as being potential fire hazards.

Typically, the electrical service panel for a house is located in the garage. This makes it easy to check the panel for service voltage to the house and determine whether there are unused circuits. If circuits are available, they can be dedicated to the garage workshop. For example, if there are three 20-amp breaker circuits not in use, one could be used for lighting, another for the table saw and the third for outlets for hand power tools. An alternative option is to install a second electrical panel that is separate from the house electrical service, often referred to as a *subpanel*. The subpanel consists of circuit breakers dedicated to the workshop. Subpanels are relatively easy to install; however, call a licensed electrician if you have any reservations about your ability to handle the installation.

Almost as important as adequate electrical power is the loca-

tion of the electrical outlets. There is consensus among woodworkers that outlets should be everywhere in the room, including the ceiling. My suggestion is to first design the location of cabinets, the workbench and machines, and then determine the location of outlets. There should be outlets at either end of the workbench and approximately 5' apart around the open walls. And don't forget to place several outlets at overhead locations near the workbench. Some woodworkers prefer having all outlets approximately 4' from the floor; others prefer lower outlets so that the cords aren't suspended in the air.

Why so many outlets? It's simple: so you can avoid potentially annoying electrical tool scenarios. If there are too few outlets in the workshop area, you will either be constantly plugging and unplugging AC cords while you work, or you will be tempted to use extension cords with multiple sockets, which could potentially damage your tools because the correct voltage is not being supplied.

It's better to have outlets at the ends of a workbench so that power cords are near you and away from the work area. Electrical cords positioned over a workbench can easily smear wet glue and scatter glue bottles, screws and smaller tools as you work with a tool and drag the cord back and forth. AC cords on a workbench also can be accidentally cut or damaged by belt sanders, routers and jigsaws. Finally, an adequate number of outlets means less opportunity for cords to become tangled or to be a problem for foot travel.

Electrical wiring in unfinished basements is simplified if the joists are exposed and there is no ceiling. Finished basements will require remodeling to locate and place new wiring. The type of wiring and conduit used will vary with different building codes. Generally, wiring is routed through the joists and installed in conduit when the wires are routed down the wall surfaces. I would suggest that you select conduit that, while meeting code requirements, is also tough enough to resist being bumped by lumber and other heavy objects. I had electrical contractors install wiring and lights in my workshop in Syracuse, New York: They drilled holes in the joists and installed Romex cables from the subpanel to both the lights and the 110V and 220V outlet locations. Rigid conduit was used from the top of the basement wall to the outlet location.

Installing Adequate Lighting

Very often lighting is set up haphazardly; that is, the local hardware store will have a sale on 4'-long fluorescent lights, and so these become the workshop lights. Attached to rafters, they are turned on via a pull string. While this does produce light, there are better approaches.

The lighting possibilities for garage workshops are more numerous than those for basements because of the ease of access to natural light through walls, the ceiling and the garage door. If the garage window is too small, it can be removed and replaced with a larger one. The simplest replacement types are manufactured windows, which are available in many sizes and types. If the garage has open rafters, it's easy to install skylights. Skylights offer wonderful lighting with a quality unlike any artificial lighting. Natural light makes the color of finishing products easier to identify and use, both on and off wood. And during the winter months, the psychological lift of working in sunlight is extremely positive. Adding windows to garage doors is fairly straightforward. If the garage door is articulated, with frame and panel construction, some of the panels can be removed and replaced with either safety glass, acrylic or Plexiglas. I advise against using standard window glass because garage doors are easily bumped, and the opening and closing process usually includes some sort of impact.

House contractors usually install nothing more than a single bulb with an on/off pull string in basements. Which, of course, is totally wrong for a workshop. If the basement ceiling is finished, it's tempting to retrofit lights onto the ceiling surface. Although this is easy to accomplish, the effect is a lowered ceiling, which a hinders your efforts to move long or tall objects. Consider recessed lights in finished ceilings; if the basement ceiling is unfinished, install 4' or 8' fluorescent lights between ceiling joists.

Adequate Shop Ventilation

Fresh air is of paramount importance in a workshop. Not only do you require clean air for breathing, but air that is too wet, dry, dusty or stale affects the quality of the woodworking project. Poor air causes finishes to not adhere or set up properly. Wet air causes wood to expand (and later shrink when moved to a drier area), as well as rust and stain tools and machines. Stale air contains assorted pollutants that affect wood, tools, finishes—and woodworkers.

The simplest ventilation system is windows and doors. However, some caution is in order. Open windows and doors lead to a degree of interaction with the outside world. Noise and dust will leave the shop and visit the neighborhood. Bugs seem to quickly find open shop doors and may bite you, leave tracks on freshly varnished surfaces or burrow into stacks of wood and lay millions of eggs. Open windows and doors broadcast the fact that you are a woodworker. While this may be a good form of advertising, you may not want to tell the world that you have expensive tools and machines.

If a ventilation system is deemed a worthy investment for both woodworking and health reasons, it's prudent to consult with ventilation specialists. A system should be designed to bring a continuous flow of fresh air into the shop and to filter the exhausted air. This type of ventilation system is usually designed for a specific shop: No off-the-shelf systems are available. A basic unit will cost between $1000 and $2000.

If you decide to install a ventilation fan unit, the type found in most home improvement centers, there are a few cautions. Be certain that the fan motor is explosionproof and dustproof. Solvents such as lacquer thinner, alcohol, acetone and paint thinner are very flammable. When these solvents become fumes and are airborne, they are still flammable. It is very dangerous to vent fumes through a fan motor that could spark or that is not

made for venting flammable solvents. Fine dust is also highly flammable and potentially explosive, so enclosed motors that are designed for use around dust should be used.

Also consider that when cold outside air is brought into the shop, the warm inside air is exhausted. If the workshop is heated, that means higher heating bills due to the constant loss of warm air as it is vented from the shop.

In this day and age, you simply cannot vent fumes and dust into the outside environment without some repercussions. Even home woodshops must—or should—abide by community air quality directives and laws. Furthermore, neighbors generally are not tolerant of noise, dust and clouds of fumes invading their space.

Heating the Shop

Heating the workshop is a difficult issue. Working in a warm room is often thought of as a luxury, because heating units are potentially dangerous around woodworking solvents and materials, and because a separate heating unit or system is thought of as too expensive. If you live in a warm climate, heating the workshop might not be necessary. However, a warm, dry workshop will stabilize humidity, keeping lumber at a constant

moisture content; the warm air will also help prevent rust. Always check local building codes and with your local fire department regarding the installation of heating units in the workshop.

Don't Overlook Shop Security

Fear and worry are different conditions. *Fear* is a natural reaction to a terrible and immediate situation; *worry* is self-manufactured nervousness. Secure your garage workshop with common sense. There are a number of devices and procedures to keep everything safe: installing door locks and dead bolts; closing doors and windows; installing machine on/off switch locks; shutting off the circuit breakers to the workshop; maintaining a low profile and minimizing noise (unwanted advertising); knowing your neighbors; not loaning tools; keeping fire extinguishers and first-aid kits handy; and keeping a list of emergency telephone numbers near the telephone.

BASEMENT WOODSHOPS

I've had basement workshops for many years, and I can say that, although there were many good things about the location, there were also some disadvantages. However, the basement is a reasonable workshop location, especially if you want to park cars, boats and motorcycles in the garage.

A small gas furnace is located in the corner of this workshop. There are no flammable materials close to the furnace.

First, the benefits: The basement workshop that is accessed through the house is generally more secure and less apparent to the outside world than a garage. Noise isn't as likely to bother the neighbors. Basement workshops are warmer during the winter months, and it is both easy and comfortable to work in a basement workshop at any time of day. For example, on especially hot summer days, basements offer a wonderful escape from the heat. Since there are no large windows and doors, there can be generous amounts of wall storage. Unlike a garage, which is constantly used for storage and foot travel, the basement is somewhat out of the main pathways and can usually be sealed off by closing a single door.

The main problems with basement workshops are access, stairs, overhead height, ventilation, noise and dust. Moving lumber, heavy machines and finished constructions in and out of basements can be difficult because of basement stairs, hallways, corners, doors and less-than-straight-line pathways to the basement. Moving heavy objects can be further complicated by floor-to-ceiling heights, especially in stairways and around heating ducts, pipes, lights and other overhead projections.

Consider Access to a Basement Shop

A typical basement might be accessed from the kitchen, often via a hallway and several doors from the garage. If you plan on using lumber, the transportation of that lumber to the basement may well cause serious family discussions. Carrying a single 10' board can easily damage doors and door frames, floor moldings, walls, shelving, cabinets, picture frames, carpets, windows, lamps, lights and kitchen counters (along with everything on them). It's no wonder that some woodworkers have a radial arm saw in the garage for cutting boards into shorter lengths before moving them to the basement.

Installing Doors

One option for basement access is to install an exterior hatch or cellar door. If your basement already has a cellar door, you are set. However, if you are considering the installation of one, several factors must be considered. The cellar door requires its own foundation, normally to the same depth as the basement. That means that a hole approximately 8′ × 8′ × 10′ will need to be dug, which may compromise existing drainage systems. The cellar door area should not interfere with plumbing pipes and electrical cables, and should be placed where the grade is the lowest and slopes away from the foundation of the house.

Cellar doors are easier to install if your basement is constructed of cinder block, brick or stone. I considered having a cellar door installed in our basement. Because the basement walls were solid concrete, I consulted a cellar door specialist. He said the job wouldn't be a problem, but as we proceeded to discuss details a few red flags appeared. It would be necessary to use diamond saws to score the concrete, and both the sawing and the subsequent sledge hammer work would produce volumes of fine dust that would

travel throughout the house. We decided that the work area could be isolated with plastic sheeting, but I wasn't thrilled with the idea of concrete dust floating around my stationary machines (downstairs) or my wife's kitchen (upstairs). However, what finally killed the project was that the contractor told me to remove all hanging lamps and wall-hung items from the entire house. When I asked why, he replied that the basement walls were about 12 years old and well hardened, and that the sledge hammer work would not only rattle the entire house but also pop out drywall nails throughout it. That did it. Since I wasn't willing to re-nail, replaster and repaint all the upstairs rooms, I decided that I could do without an outside entrance to the basement.

Reducing Irritants

It takes a very tolerant family to live with machinery noise just below their feet. The constant sound of dust collectors, the screaming sound of routers and the high-pitched whine of table saws all will travel throughout the house. Another invasive workshop material is dust. Even when

using dust collectors, dust seems to migrate to the furthest areas of the house. Fumes and odors from finishes also can permeate an entire house. Noise, dust and fumes—not the sort of things most people want to have in their home.

Be Sure to Ventilate Well

Air in a basement workshop is usually damp, dry or stale. Humidity, dust, finishing fumes, mold, mildew, air circulation and ventilation all are related problems in the basement workshop. The typical basement is more humid during the spring and summer months when the furnace isn't used; when the furnace is used, the basement dries. This alternating cycle of humidity and dryness will affect lumber and joinery by either swelling or shrinking the wood. The only effective method of moderating this cycle is to adequately moderate the air quality. Typically, the things that can be done are to cover sump pump holes, seal basement walls with sealers and basement paints, provide good air ventilation from the outside (windows and fans) and operate dehumidifiers all year long.

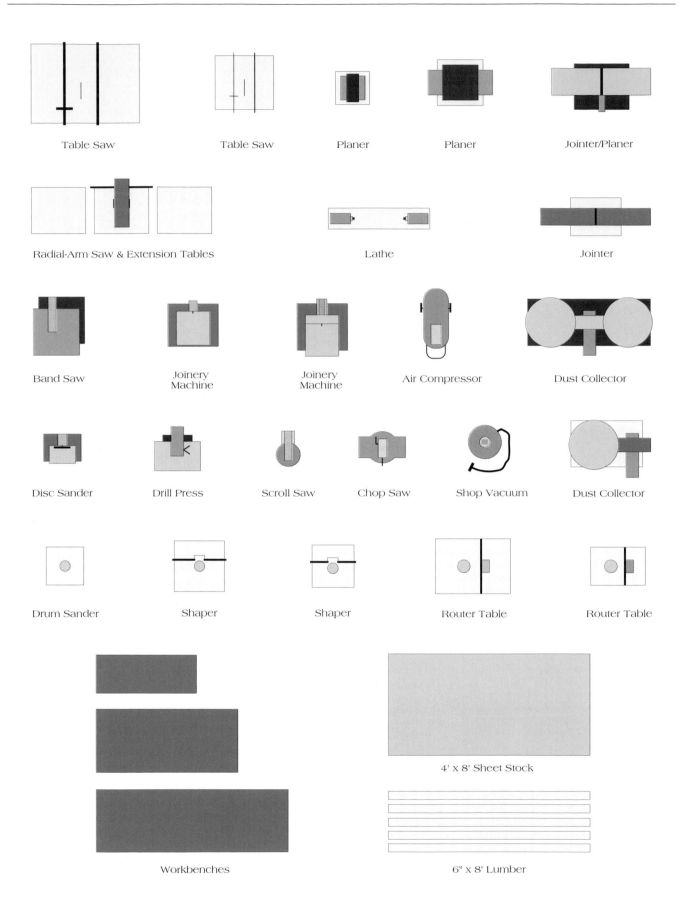

Table Saw

Table Saw

Planer

Planer

Jointer/Planer

Radial-Arm Saw & Extension Tables

Lathe

Jointer

Band Saw

Joinery Machine

Joinery Machine

Air Compressor

Dust Collector

Disc Sander

Drill Press

Scroll Saw

Chop Saw

Shop Vacuum

Dust Collector

Drum Sander

Shaper

Shaper

Router Table

Router Table

Workbenches

4' x 8' Sheet Stock

6" x 8' Lumber

3

MAXIMIZING YOUR SHOP SPACE

◼

Be comfortable and enjoy the locale. Personalize the workshop; it's not an industrial facility.

Imagine an empty college dormitory consisting of 100 rooms. Each of those rooms has the same dimensional configuration, and each has the same basic furniture. Now fill those rooms with college students and wait a month. After a few weeks, those rooms will no longer resemble each other. The unique personalization process will make it difficult to imagine the original sameness of the basic rooms. Individualism, personal interests, budgets, creativity and experience are just some of the factors that shape those rooms. The same is true in workshops. If 100 woodworkers were given the same room in which to create workshops,

there would be 100 variations on workshop layout.

DESIGN WITH "YOU" IN MIND

Fundamentally, the layout of your shop should be comfortable and reflect your personal style of woodworking. While it's interesting to study another woodworker's workshop, you must always relate what you see to your own needs, tools, materials and room location. Ultimately, the ideal workshop is the one in which you are comfortable. Personal satisfaction is one of the main reasons for woodworking. There are too many references to the *perfect* workshop in books and magazines; when I see these workshops, I always feel that they are impersonal and lack character and individuality. Ironically,

when only you know what's on cluttered shelves and in boxes of odd and ends, or what a curious jig-type object is for, you have achieved that unique workshop that is *yours*. The perfect workshop is a concept, not a real place.

USING THE WORK TRIANGLE

A designer fad that surfaces occasionally is the *work triangle*. The triangle concept is frequently applied to kitchen layout; that is, the relationship between sink, refrigerator and range. The best work triangle configuration is when the sides of the triangle are equal (or nearly equal) and the total length of the sides is 14 to 22 feet. This preliminary design layout has some merit when it is applied to the workshop, if for no

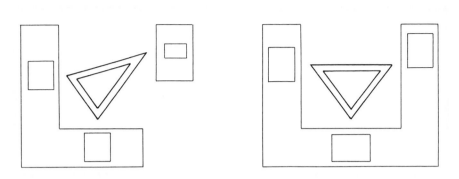

Typical work triangles showing work area layout and triangular pattern of motion between work locations.

other reason than to determine principal work areas and efficient placement of workstations and storage locations. If the work triangle becomes too large or strangely shaped, it may be necessary to reorganize the work area layout. For example, it's of little value to have hand tool storage too far from the workbench, or to have tools in an awkward location. Likewise, certain tools, machines and accessories should be located so that the operator can comfortably use them in interrelated processes (for example, a bench grinder and a lathe).

In the workshop, it's important to create a layout that is both comfortable for the woodworker and efficient. However, the work pathway might be circular, triangular or another shape. What is important is to design a layout in which there's a relationship among various work areas, traffic patterns, windows, doors and all the other features of a room. For example, many woodworkers

might think that the workbench is the principal focal point in the workshop. If that is so, machines, tools and accessories that are used the most should be in a direct pathway to the workbench. In this case, in addition to a conveniently placed hand-tool storage area, a drill press, miter saw and band saw, which are the significantly used machines, would be located five to ten feet away from the workbench. The secondary machines—a jointer, table saw or joinery machine—would be slightly further from the workbench. Basic to the primary and secondary work patterns are factors such as being able to

move lumber freely or to avoid stepping on cables, air hoses, and dust collector hoses.

BASING LAYOUT ON SEQUENTIAL WORK FLOW

Often, the experts refer to the notion that work should be done sequentially; that is, woodworking procedures can—and should— be done in a methodical, step-by-step sequence.

1. Rough lumber is cut to length with radial arm saw.
2. Rough lumber pieces are flattened, smoothed and thicknessed with a planer.
3. Rough edges are smoothed and straightened with jointer.
4. Semifinished lumber is re-sawn with a band saw.
5. Re-sawn wood is smoothed with a jointer and planer.
6. Smoothed pieces are cut to specific lengths and widths with a table saw.
7. Joinery is done to workpieces with hand tools, a router and so on.

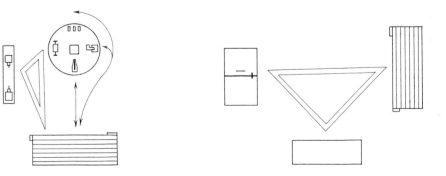

Work triangle that includes workbench, lathe and round work surface mounted on post. Work triangle between workbench, cabinet and table saw.

8. Workpieces are glued and clamped.
9. Glued-up assembly is sanded.
10. Finish is applied.

If this sequence is properly followed, the layout of machines, tools, accessories and work areas would be ranked (or used) in this order:

1. radial arm saw
2. workbench
3. planer
4. workbench
5. jointer
6. workbench
7. bandsaw
8. jointer
9. planer
10. workbench
11. table saw
12. workbench
13. joinery tools
14. workbench
15. assembly and gluing
16. sanding
17. finishing

RELATING MACHINE FUNCTION TO LAYOUT CONSIDERATIONS

The significant features of the sequential-use list are that the workbench is used repeatedly and that most machines are used for particular (limited) functions. The radial arm saw is used for cutting lumber to length, the planer is used for thicknessing and smoothing boards, the jointer is used for squaring edges, the band saw is used for making different thicknesses of lumber (resawing), the table saw is used for the final sizing of boards and joinery machines are used for cutting joints (i.e., dovetail mortises and tenons). If this process is followed as a regular routine, it can be used as a template for woodshop layout.

Start With Initial Cutting

Start with the premise that lumber and sheet materials should be near the workshop entry door; that way it won't be necessary to move heavy and awkward materials through the workshop. Station the initial cutting machine—probably the radial arm saw, panel saw or sawhorses and a circular saw—near the lumber and sheet material storage.

If a radial arm saw is set up on a long table placed against a wall, the area beneath the saw is often used for storage. I have seen several useful adaptations of this space: storage for roll-around cabinet modules, fixed cabinets and drawers and open-shelf storage for shorter pieces of wood. The size and shape of the workshop affects which style of storage is used. In large rooms the radial arm saw is usually some distance from the main work area. This generally makes fixed cabinets and drawers less appealing, because of the walking distance, and makes open-shelf storage more attractive. If the workshop is small and compact, the use of modular cabinets maximizes storage and tool usage.

Facing Materials

Once lumber is cut to a manageable length, the planer is used. The planer requires an open work space on either side. The open area is defined by the length of the longest lumber that will enter and exit the planer. The traditional stationary planer is large and heavy, and is usually oriented on the long axis of the workshop. The new suitcase (or lunch box) size planers are lightweight, portable and easily moved to an open area. Since the concept of a portable planer is relatively new, most traditional woodworkers haven't gotten accustomed to the idea that the planer can be stored on a shelf when it's not being used. Newer woodworkers, however, are beginning to use the planer somewhat like a router or circular saw, taking it from the shelf when it's needed and then storing it away.

The jointer is often located against an uncluttered wall because, like the planer, it requires an open area for infeed and outfeed clearance. The most common jointers have 6"-wide cutter heads and 3'–4' bed lengths. Both planer and jointer are far more efficient if the machines

Hannes Hase has a commercial business making windows and doors, and his workshop is in an odded-shaped and odd-sized room. He uses a Felder combination machine that includes a table saw, jointer and planer.

The Felder machine rotates upon a swivel base so that each function is easily accessible. Note that the planer tables are raised.

have cutter heads that are the same width. Oddly, very few planers and jointers are made this way, even when they are from the same manufacturer. This is based upon the (relic) premise that jointers are used for edges, and planers are used for surface widths. In reality, the best method for preparing boards (to make them flat) is to first smooth and flatten one board surface on a wide jointer. Once the surface is flat, place the flat surface against the planer's flat surface and feed the board into the planer so that the rough side is smoothed by the cutter. This produces dimensionally flat wood, free of twists, cups and distortions. If rough lumber is fed directly into a planer without having one flattened surface, the surfaces will be planed smooth,

but the board will have any twists or cups originally found in the rough lumber. The only machine solution for this woodworking dilemma is to have a wide-surface jointer. Unfortunately, these machines are rather heavy, large and expensive. A worthwhile alternative is the combination jointer and planer. The advantage to this type of combination machine is twofold. First, you have one machine instead of two. Second, a variety of combination machines with cutter head widths from 10″ to 24″ are available, making it much easier to work with wider boards.

The basic design of the jointer/planer combination machines incorporates over and under the cutter head use: Jointing and flattening work is done on the top surface of the machine,

as on a standard jointer; planing is accomplished by feeding the board under the table and into the lower area of the cutter head. I strongly recommend the combination jointer/planer, especially if workshop space is limited and you want dimensionally flat and stable boards.

The band saw has several valuable applications, including cutting curved edges and re-sawing. Re-sawing is possibly the most useful application, if only because it is nearly impossible with any other machine. However, re-sawing lumber requires adequate space for the lumber to enter and exit the band saw. Typically, the band saw is positioned near a wall so that the cutting direction is parallel to the wall. However, if the band saw is too close to the wall, it's difficult to

Secondary Cutting and Shaping

The doors behind the band saw are opened when re-sawing is done.

use the machine for cutting curves because the workpiece will most likely rotate into the wall. One interesting solution is locating the band saw in front of a door. When re-sawing long lumber is necessary, the door is opened and the cuts are made.

PLACING A TABLE SAW The location of the table saw requires careful consideration. The table saw is generally used as both a primary and secondary processing machine. Primarily, it is used to cut long, wide boards to smaller lengths, or to cut full-size sheets of man-made materials to smaller sizes. Secondary work consists of the final shaping of boards, cutting joints, grooves, dadoes and moulding profiles. Each of these elements has specific design requirements. Primary processing requires adequate area around the table saw to permit the handling of large boards and sheets. This means that there should be both infeed and outfeed space for the safe handling of materials. Under no circumstances should material bump, or be deflected by, surrounding tables, cabinets

or other workshop items. The operator should have absolute control of large pieces while using the table saw. Many experienced woodworkers attach support tables on either side and on the outfeed side of the table saw to support oversize boards and sheets. Never attempt to cut a full-size sheet of plywood or particleboard on a table saw that doesn't have ancillary support tables. The sheer weight of plywood, held suspended in air over the back of the table saw by the operator, plus the spinning saw blade is an accident waiting to happen. Furthermore, using the table saw to cross-cut the ends of long boards is also foolhardy.

DO YOU NEED A SHAPER? Ten or fifteen years ago it was fairly common to find shapers as part of the standard woodshop machinery.

Tom Dailey's table saw features a mobile base and a fold-down extension table.

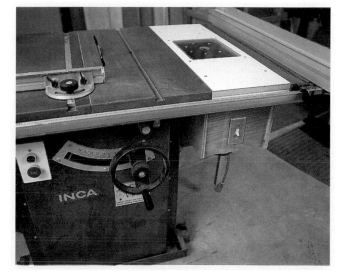

The Inca saw has a shop-made router table inserted between the saw's main table and extension. The router table is sealed, with a dust collection port mounted on the back side.

However, many new woodworkers think that the router table supplements or replaces the shaper. I don't think that the router table actually replaces the shaper, but many woodworkers rely on the router table as the principal machine for making dadoes and grooves, shaping edges, joinery and frame and panel constructions. Part of the reason for this popularity is that there are many magazine articles featuring router tables: The router is a very popular tool and there are hundreds of different router bits. The sophistication of the router is a modern success story. Plunge routers with variable speeds and 2 to 5 hp are now very common. And there are now routers specifically designed to work upside down under a router table.

The shaper as a machine of choice has fallen out of favor because of several factors. The shaper hasn't changed all that much during this time of the router table development, and many hobby woodworkers feel that the shaper is more dangerous than a router table. This fear, distrust and rejection of shapers is, I think, based upon several perceptions: Shapers have large cutters that make large cuts, thus appearing more aggressive (i.e., more dangerous); shaper cutters are more expensive than router bits, and shapers are more expensive than routers; common

router functions are improved and made easier when done with router tables; and shapers are associated with professional cabinet shops—they haven't been marketed to hobby woodworkers. Actually, there are several important and real differences between the two machines. One of the main differences is that, excluding special adapters, shaper cutters are designed to cut board edges. Also, shapers operate in the 6000 to 10,000 RPM range; variable-speed routers run at 8000 to 24,000 RPM. And, the more professional shaper models have tilting spindles, forward and reverse switches and interchangeable ½", ¾", 1" and 1½" spindles.

WILL A ROUTER TABLE DO? Router tables allow both edge work and board-surface work. However, in spite of the large-diameter router bit trend, routers are limited to ¼", ⅜" and ½" shanks. Even with a router set at 8000 RPM, I have never felt comfortable using 2" (or greater) diameter router bits. If I do use one, I make many light passes, raising the bit ever so slightly until the final cut is made. In my opinion, router tables are very useful with piloted bits and for cutting dadoes, grooves, rabbets, finger joints and other light cuts requiring cutter bit diameters of ¾" or less.

PLACING A SHAPER OR ROUTER TABLE
Whether it's a shaper or a router

Dean Bershaw's cabinetmaker's table saw features an oversized table area. This permanently installed table makes the handling and cutting of sheet materials much easier. The table is large enough to also support a planer.

Doug Matthews added a modest-size table to his table saw. Note how the Workmate holds an outfeed roller at the back of the table saw.

The Multi-Router joinery machine with custom-made dust hookup.

table, there are several important layout considerations. Both of these machines require space for moving wood in and away from the machines. And they both require rock-solid stability: Under no circumstances should these machines be wobbly or unbalanced when they are used. Many shapers feature right-angle feet attachments so that they are easily bolted to the floor. I have seen few router tables bolted to the floor, and yet they are used to cut grooves in 8' lengths of plywood. Just imagine the suspended weight of this type of wood as it exits the cutter and is hanging on the outfeed side of the router table. Shapers are generally con-structed with the motor located in the lower areas of the body, creating a lower center of gravity that helps to stabilize the machine. In order to stabilize router tables, the framework or body should be as large as possible. If you are making a router table out of plywood, adding drawers near the floor (and filling them with tools) will enhance stability. Tim Hewitt at HTC (makers of metal mobile bases) has sold many bases for both shapers and router tables. His product stabilizes these machines because the mobile base has three wheels externally located on a welded metal frame. The location of the wheels is important be-cause being outside of the machine and frame increases the footprint size of the machine. HTC has had no complaints or problems relating to shaper or router table stability.

Both machines have three active sides—the infeed, the outfeed and an open side—that all require that the adjacent areas be clear of obstructions. The fourth side, the side behind the fence, is usually positioned near a wall. Shaper and router table space requirements are determined by the length of workpieces. If, for example, frame-and-panel cabinet doors are the only thing made, the clear area should be no less than 4' on the three active sides.

However, if you are shaping or routing entry door pieces or floor-to-ceiling cabinet sides, the clear area for the infeed and outfeed directions should be at least 10'.

Using a Joinery Machine

The joinery machine is relatively new to the woodworking world, but, because of its usefulness, it's being found in more and more workshops. This machine has a router mounted horizontally and permits cutting action along X, Y and Z axes. That is, the horizontal router can be moved up and down, and the table holding the workpiece moves in and out and side to side. These machines allow for the efficient cutting of mortises and tenons, dovetails, finger joints and such. Because this machine is used for joinery, the workpieces are shorter and smaller, thus not requiring large open areas around the machine. I have been using a Multi-Router joinery machine mounted on a mobile base so that I can move it from a storage area to a suitable work area. In fact, a joinery machine probably is easier to manage when it's near the workbench. If, for example, you are making a set of six ladderback chairs, that translates into 102 pieces, 156 mortises and 156 tenons. That's quite a few pieces to keep tidy. The workbench is ideal for sorting, organizing and keeping track of all the pieces and their joinery

situation. The only drawback to this machine is that the horizontally mounted router flings dust and chips over a wide area, like a geyser of dust. If you plan on using this machine near clean areas, I would suggest that you construct some sort of dust collection device. Factor the location of a joinery machine into your layout and provide for a 4" or 5" flexible dust collection hose to dangle directly over the router bit area. That way, the discharged debris will be caught while it's airborne. Normally, dust collector ductwork is attached to specific machines and is rarely dangled near the workbench. If you do place a dangling collection hose near the workbench, be certain to add an open/close gate or a large plug at the end of the hose: There is no reason to have an open hose anywhere in the woodshop, especially near the workbench.

MOVING AROUND THE SHOP

Once the sawing, planing and joinery are finished, all that is left are the final stages of woodworking: assembly, gluing, sanding and finishing. These stages all require space for your movement while working and calm space while the workpiece is glued, clamped and finished.

Open Up Space With Mobile Tools

Most small workshops have tightly organized space, with

walkways, and little open space. Yet, assembly and finishing require open space. Generally, the solution is to move equipment out of the way to open up space; moving equipment can be facilitated if machines are mounted on mobile bases. However, heavy machines without mobile bases probably shouldn't be moved. Dragging a machine across the workshop will most likely injure you and damage the machine and the floor. Commercially made mobile bases are available for just about any machine. HTC Co. has a catalog offering a comprehensive supply of well-made bases for any type and brand of tool. They also will make customized bases for older, or unique, machines.

If tools and machines are

Custom stand for jointer and sander in the Dailey workshop. Note the dust collection system.

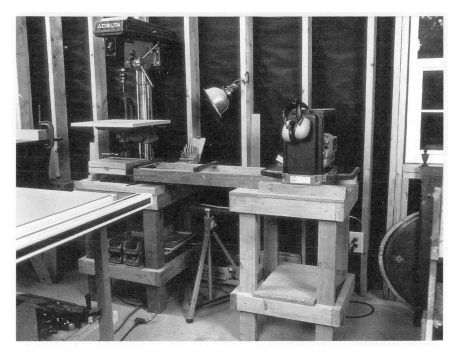

Simple work stands for planer and drill press.

small or there is sufficient room area, it's very easy to make custom stands. These are made to fit both the machine and the work area. As often as not in well-used woodshops, these stands are utilitarian and very well made.

Focus on the Workbench to Save Space

Another common assembly solution is to use the workbench for the final woodworking steps. The problem with using the workbench for assembly, gluing and finishing is that workbenches aren't necessarily wide enough for some furniture and cabinet constructions. And the workpiece is usually too high for comfortable work. A workbench height of 12″ to 24″ is ideal for assembling furniture; however,

a bench at this height is useless for many other projects. A simple solution is to have low sawhorses to temporarily support a sheet of plywood, particleboard or MDF. Assembly and clamping require a flat surface, so the sheet material should rest as flat as possible on the sawhorses. I've seen many workshops that have the sheet material attached (with screws) to a simple frame, which is often nothing more than four edge pieces and several cross-frame pieces. When it's not in use, the flat-surface assembly can be leaned against a wall or used as a catchall for general workshop use. Once the sheet material is worn out (chipped, gouged, dried glue spots, etc.), simply flip it over, use the other side until it too is

hopeless and then replace it with a fresh sheet.

Plan for Glue-Up and Assembly Space

Regarding the static time that occurs while a workpiece is being clamped, I have bruised myself more during this time than during the entire construction process. Why? I think it's because I've lowered my guard. While sawing, planing and so on, I am very focused on what I'm doing. But after the workpiece is clamped up and just sitting there, I'm usually cleaning up, putting tools away and not paying much attention to that clamp handle protruding out into the walkway. Therefore, leg and hip bruises. The moral of this tale of clumsiness is that the clamped workpiece requires space that should be as out of the way as possible. Or, you could simply leave the room while the glue dries.

DON'T FORGET ABOUT CEILING HEIGHT

So far, workshop layout has mainly focused on floor area. The other dimension that should be factored into layout plans is floor-to-ceiling height. While it may be impossible to increase the height within an existing woodshop, there are several things that you can do to maximize floor-to-ceiling height.

The most troublesome

feature of workshop height is the difficulty involved in moving long boards. Even if you are primarily lathe turning, carving or doing other small-scale projects, there will be times when lifting lumber is required. Lifting and transporting lumber is further complicated by the location and height of machines, workbenches, hanging objects and storage units. Furthermore, light fixtures are often lower than the ceiling. Moving an 8'-long board can make you feel as if you are jousting with the dark knight—or battering down the castle!

Obviously, if you are designing a new workshop, the simplest thing to do is to increase the floor-to-ceiling height. Ceiling heights of up to 12' will make almost any woodworking easier. When a new house is being built over a basement of concrete blocks, inquire about having one or two additional rows added to the basement walls so that there will be more overhead room. (I'm sure the additional construction expense will be negated when you use the basement woodshop, and the additional height will probably increase the value of your house.)

Dealing With Low Ceilings

If you are setting up your workshop in an existing garage or basement, there are several methods of dealing with standard room height.

1. Recess all light fixtures flush to the ceiling.
2. If fluorescent lights are suspended below the ceiling, install the fluorescent lights in commercially available clear safety tubes (if the light is broken, the glass shards remain in the plastic tube).
3. Remove or minimize all objects that hang from the ceiling.
4. Position machines and storage units next to a wall when moving long items. Having an open center area in the woodshop will facilitate moving long lumber.
5. Rough cut long lumber outside of the workshop.
6. If there's a window, use it for negotiating long lumber into the workshop.
7. If the ceiling is paneled or finished, consider removing the ceiling material so that the rafters are exposed. The open area between rafters, especially above the workbench area, is useful for maneuvering boards. The exposed rafters also permit additional storage and places to hang items. Dust collector ducts, air lines and wiring can be routed above the rafters to avoid cluttering the ceiling.

PLANNING FOR DUST COLLECTION

No matter how the final woodworking stages are done, the process affects the entire workshop and perhaps even the nearby living quarters. The most obvious by-product of this stage is dust and finishing product fumes. Also, the workshop generally isn't used while a workpiece is being clamped or while finished products are drying. These factors affect workshop layout in that dust and fumes can be minimized by proper collection and ventilation. Therefore, it makes sense to arrange the workshop so that sanding dust and fumes don't migrate beyond the work area. Keep both dust collectors and sanding and finishing areas away from doors and windows. Attempt to design the layout so that dust doesn't travel more than 12" away from the work area. Minimizing dust, besides keeping the living quarters in harmony, also makes applying finishes easier. There is nothing more tedious than having to clean the entire woodshop and then waiting for all airborne dust to settle before applying a finish. (In fact, the popularity of oil finishes may well be related to this situation.)

4

CUSTOMIZING YOUR WOODSHOP

There is no formula for the ideal workshop: There is you, your requirements, your budget and your expertise. Don't get side-tracked by the unnecessary.

Sam Maloof, a great American woodworker, tells a story about being approached many years ago by several very earnest engineers. They had slide rules (definitely pre-calculators), protractors, tape measures and clipboards filled with charts. Their quest was to determine the proper heights, widths, lengths and shapes to construct the ideal chair. They wanted to interview Sam about his chairs, because Sam made the most comfortable wood chairs around. (In my opinion, they are even more comfortable than upholstered and pillowed chairs.) These bright and well-meaning engineers were looking for a formula, a template or a system of shapes and angles for building something that would apply to everyone. Sam was amused by their questions, because he didn't have a formula or a chart for building his chairs.

He told them he built a chair by instinct: He sat in it, and if he was comfortable, he felt the chair owner would also be comfortable. The young engineers left, pondering that *organic* approach to chair design.

Luthier Robert Girdis has used a small room to make beautiful guitars for many years.

NO TWO SHOPS ARE ALIKE

This story relates to designing woodworking shops because I've never met two woodworkers that have workshops of the same shape or size. Nor have I met two woodworkers that have the same tools, machines, lumber pile or specific woodworking style. And these differences exist even though woodworkers tend to read the same books and magazines. There are simply too many personal features, bud-

Robert Girdis built a mock-up of his "ideal" workshop.

gets, locations, and room configurations for there to be significant similarities between workshops—or for me to say there is a uniform workshop design. I know a lathe turner who specializes in turning miniature objects, and yet his workshop is large enough to park an airplane in. I also know woodworkers who have full shops in single-car, low-ceiling garages and are building plywood cases and cabinets. To illustrate one very simple problem in generalizing workshop design, suppose that two woodworkers have bought exactly the same tools and plan on setting up a workshop in order to build exactly the same wood projects. The only difference is their workshop configuration: one is a 12′×30′ rectangle with two doors and windows on three walls; the other is a 19′×19′ square with no windows and

only one door. Even though both workshops have approximately 360 square feet, it doesn't take much to visualize that wall storage, machine placement and overhead lighting will be very different for the two workshops. Windows and a second door create such limitations that only creatively designed storage units are effective.

What *is* appropriate for designing a woodshop is considering a standard set of variables that more or less apply to every workshop. Sort of the "food, clothes and shelter" basics of the workshop. For workshops, these elements would be available: workshop location, interest, finances, machinery, tools and storage.

CHECK OUT OTHER SHOPS

Study existing workshops. In spite of the inevitable differences

Corner and workbench in the Girdis workshop.

The Girdis workshop under construction. Workshop is located on house property.

Doug Matthews built a barn-shaped workshop to visually fit the rural setting where he lives. Note that his home is located near the workshop. Doug restores and repairs antique furniture and has just set up a showroom in the workshop's second-floor area to display and sell antique furniture.

Exterior view of Steve Balter's workshop.

with your future workshop, existing workshops do offer ideas and potential problem-solving solutions. Study machine locations, especially their relationship to other machines and open space (work areas). Note the location of workbenches and storage areas for frequently used tools. Other principal concerns are lumber storage, finishing supply storage, finishing areas, clamp storage, electrical outlets, dust collection ducts and openings. Ask "Why did you do that?" and take note of any response.

Start With People You Know
To find workshops, first talk with friends and neighbors who do woodworking. Because they are friends and neighbors, you prob-

ably can trust their advice. Joining local woodworking clubs and guilds is also a great source of information. Generally, woodworkers join these clubs to share information. And you will find that, because most of them have gone through the struggle of designing workshops, they aren't shy about sharing their solutions.

Look at Schools and Pro Shops
Schools and professional woodworking shops, although tempting as sources of information, aren't necessarily useful for home-workshop applications. That's because schools and professionals don't have the same purposes, room sizes, machines and tools, budgets and interests as the home woodworker. A

school might be a repository of machinery valued by teachers with specific points of view; the professional woodshop might rely on expensive processing machines, with no hand tool applications whatsoever. Having said that, if the opportunity arises for you to visit these workshops, do it, and then use the information as a benchmark of a different woodworking evolution.

Additional Shops to Check Out
Other workshops that might offer some value, if for no other reason than studying storage solutions, air filtration and workbenches, are artists' studios and the shops of jewelers, painters and auto mechanics. These workshops will have single-purpose applications, yet each offers unique problem-solving solutions. As

you study these shops, remember that your workshop will be generalized in nature, but how a sculptor or mechanic stores tools can be invaluable information.

MAKE YOUR MASTER PLAN

After you have conceptualized your workshop design, it's time to make a master plan. The master plan is a general plan of room size, potential features and tools. These are, in turn, filtered through your woodworking discipline and style. Create this plan with as much intensity and enthusiasm as possible, as if you are designing a kitchen or a master bedroom. Of course, the master plan can be changed as you proceed with developing your workshop, but it is the ideal starting point, the first visualization of your future workshop.

Choose Your Tooling and Storage

Make a list of all the machines, tools and storage areas that you ultimately want.

FURNITURE OR CABINETRY SHOP If you want to build furniture, consider:
- Workbench
- Table saw
- Band saw
- Router table or shaper
- Jointer
- Planer
- Drill press
- Disc/belt sander

- Joinery machine
- Dust collector
- Scroll saw
- Air compressor

Also consider storage cabinets and shelves for:
- Routers
- Drills
- Sanders
- Spray equipment
- Air tools
- Biscuit joiner
- Clamps
- Hand tools
- Finishing supplies
- Lumber, plywood and small pieces of wood

WOODCARVING SHOP
- Workbench
- Band saw
- Grinder (or a powered sharpening device)
- Disc/belt sander
- Dust collector
- Scroll saw
- Drill press

And storage cabinets and shelves for:
- Rotary carving tools
- Sanders
- Burrs and bits for rotary tool
- Hand tools (carving chisels and mallets)
- Lumber and small pieces of wood
- Clamps
- Drills
- Finishing supplies

WOOD TURNING SHOP
- Lathe
- Workbench

- Band saw
- Drill press
- Dust collector
- Grinder (or a powered sharpening device)

And storage cabinets and shelves for:
- Lathe tools
- Drills
- Sanders
- Sanding supplies and sandpaper
- Lathe accessories
- Hand tools
- Finishing supplies
- Lumber, blocks, logs and small pieces of wood

MISCELLANEOUS NEEDS List all other important features that are useful for any workshop.
- Electrical service panel
- Electrical outlets (110V and 220V)
- Plumbing (sinks, toilets and so on)
- Secondary lighting (spotlights)
- Windows
- Doors
- Containers for scrap wood

Design the Workshop on Paper

Use ¼″ grid paper and a scale of ¼″ = 1′. First, draw the shape of the potential workshop. Include all permanent elements of the room, such as support beams, steps and water heaters. On another sheet of paper, draw representational shapes of all machines, shelves and storage units and cut them out with scissors. Now, try the cutouts in different locations on the floor plan drawing. Note the way that open space or machine positions differ from your preconceptions of an idealized workshop layout. It may seem that particular machines, which should be easy to place, become difficult to locate because of windows or doors. Storage units may have to be modified from original designs because of machine placement or electrical outlets.

Designing With a Paper Grid and Paper Tools

Obviously, it's easier to move pieces of paper than machines and cabinets, and the benefits of this technique are far-reaching. Generally, the problem with home workshops is too little space, not too much space. Placing workshop items becomes a struggle toward efficiency. When arranging the paper cutouts, it might become apparent that the floor plan and machinery don't match. There may not be enough space for your needs. It may be impossible to have a comfortable blend of machines, cabinets, safe areas around machines and open work areas. The paper cutouts will aid in this discovery, which is part of the reason that you should include every possible item on the master plan list.

Don't leave out machines and workshop furniture that will be acquired in the future. Even if the purchase of something is several years off, include it in the master plan. All too often the owner of a cramped workshop will spend too much time attempting to overcome the problem of space limitations. Storage becomes convoluted, machines are too close together and, instead of working on projects, time is spent either moving things around or finding—or hiding—objects. Be prepared for future acquisitions.

Planning for the Future

Here's an issue that's complicated and somewhat vexing: How do you know how to start out compared to where you will end up? Perhaps you've seen beautiful handmade furniture, bowls and carvings at a craft fair, and this has inspired you to take up woodworking. But, you've had no woodworking lessons or experiences with other woodworkers. What do you do to get started? Let's assume that you read woodworking books and magazines, watch do-it-yourself videos and visit tool stores. All of these are very inspirationally produced by experts. But do these sources really help you to find a starting place? The question is, will you make furniture, turn bowls or carve? What if you set

up a workshop for carving and later find that lathe-turned bowls are your real interest?

Relax. When you create the master plan, realize that most machines are for general-purpose applications. Table saws and band saws aren't designed for single-purpose use. However, carving chisels and lathe tools *are* single-purpose tools. Fortunately, you can start out with a half dozen of these tools and not spend large sums of money. And if you decide that carving isn't for you, it's easy to sell them. If you aren't certain of the type of woodworking you want to pursue, initially stay as general as possible, realizing that some tools are worth purchasing, if for no other reason than for experimentation.

BUDGETING FOR SHOP SETUP

If you are setting up a workshop for the first time and have never purchased machinery, tools and supplies, don't get discouraged. I have talked with hundreds of beginning woodworkers and have heard many very similar questions. Usually beginning woodworkers have specific budget amounts and space limitations as their first priorities. These conditions are quickly followed by questions about what type of machinery and hand tools should be purchased. After these issues, questions follow about specific brands, where to purchase machinery and tools, what books and magazines are recommended and where one can find how-to and hands-on instruction. The response to these questions is like the solution to a complicated mathematics problem: Start at the beginning, do your step-by-step work on paper, and progress through every step until the solution is found.

Translating that type of formula to designing a workshop is straightforward. Suppose that your budget is $3000 for machinery and tools, the potential workshop area has 200 square feet and you are planning on generalized woodworking for yourself and your family. First, what will $3000 purchase? Make a list of possible selections. Also factor into this list whether you are planning to purchase locally or through mail-order catalogs and whether you prefer machines made in the U.S.A. or those made in foreign countries.

Prioritize Your Purchases

Obviously, both lists are over budget, and neither list includes hand tools, sharpening supplies, sandpaper, etc. The next step is to prioritize the tool list and purchase the most important items first. For general-purpose woodworking, the scroll saw and lathe may not be necessary. However,

POTENTIAL MACHINES AND COSTS

List A		List B	
cabinetmaker's table saw:	$1600	contractor's table saw:	$800
15" stationary planer:	$1000	12" portable planer:	$400
6" stationary jointer:	$1300	6" portable jointer:	$300
12" band saw:	$900	10" band saw:	$350
heavy-duty lathe:	$2000	bench-top lathe:	$450
16½" floor drill press:	$400	bench-top drill press:	$100
scroll saw:	$500	scroll saw:	$200
cyclone dust collector with duct:	$1000	2-bag dust collector on rollers:	$400
3 hp plunge router:	$280	1½ hp standard router:	$200
router table with additional router:	$400	router table only:	$100
plate joiner:	$200	plate joiner:	$200
14V cordless drill:	$210	12V cordless drill:	$185
finish sander:	$80	finish sander:	$80
4×24 belt sander:	$225	3×21 belt sander:	$170
Total:	$10,095	Total:	$3935

Tom Dailey's workshop is located in a ground-level basement. Plywood is brought in through the back door and cut with a panel saw.

design the workshop location as if all the listed machines and tool items were available. It's much easier to create the workshop layout requirements in the planning stage than to retrodesign a workshop when space is unavailable or wasn't factored into construction plans.

If you plan on cutting large amounts of plywood and can't decide between a cabinetmak-

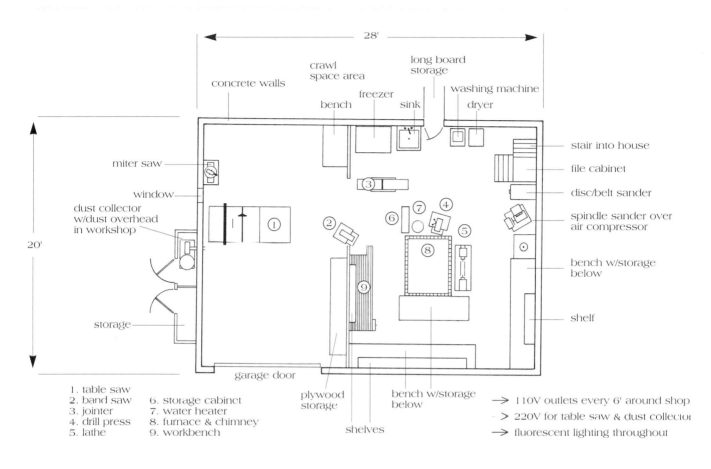

28'

20'

crawl
space area

long board
storage

concrete walls

freezer

washing machine

bench

sink

dryer

miter saw

window

dust collector
w/dust overhead
in workshop

storage

garage door

stair into house

file cabinet

disc/belt sander

spindle sander over
air compressor

bench w/storage
below

shelf

plywood
storage

bench w/storage
below

shelves

1. table saw
2. band saw
3. jointer
4. drill press
5. lathe

6. storage cabinet
7. water heater
8. furnace & chimney
9. workbench

→ 110V outlets every 6' around shop
> 220V for table saw & dust collector
→ fluorescent lighting throughout

Mark Kulseth's workshop

er's table saw (e.g., Delta's Uni-saw), because you think it would be more advantageous for this procedure, and a contractor's table saw, because it better fits your space, consider the following alternative. Size plywood into smaller sections with a circular saw or jigsaw by cutting approximately ⅛" wider than the measured layout lines and cleaning the rough-cut plywood edges using a router and a straight bit. Or construct auxiliary tables on both sides and outfeed areas of the table saw so that the plywood is manageable during cutting.

When I started woodworking, I had only vague concepts of what tools to purchase. At that time, there were no magazines devoted to woodworking, and the hardware stores were primarily devoted to the trade (i.e., contractors and builders). And twenty-some years ago, the main articles in the mechanic-type magazines were either "Table saws vs. radial arm saws" or "How to build a plywood dingy." It was difficult to find information or sources for antique tools, speciality tools, foreign-made tools or high-quality tools. Over the

years, I have purchased a variety of table saws, routers, drills and assorted gadgets. Most of my earlier purchases have been replaced with upgraded versions, and the original tools were sold through the newspaper classified section. The point is, your skills, pocketbook and interests change with time. If you know what you want now, that's great. But don't worry if you aren't sure—you will know in time. So if you can't afford a particular machine at the moment, purchase something that is affordable and upgrade later on. If you want to

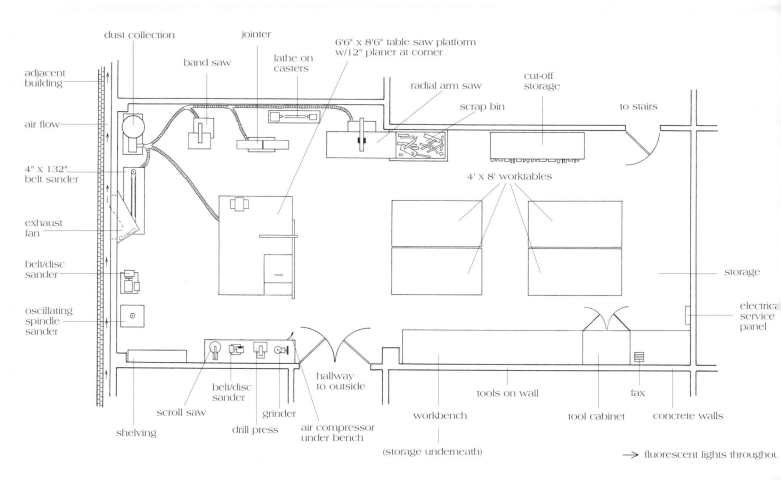

Dean Bershaw's workshop

PLANNING STORAGE

The storage in most workshops is generally haphazard. It's common to see cabinets built in odd locations because the space was unused or was too awkward for other uses. When a workshop is properly planned and designed, cabinets and shelves fit the room and present an orderliness that makes work easier. If possible, try something different, go ahead and try it. If it isn't right for you, it's easy to resell most tools.

construct storage cabinets in modular units. A set of smaller cabinets is easier to build and easier to move within the room. For example, a 9'-long wall is available for cabinets. It's conceivable that one 9' cabinet could be installed. However, it's difficult to build something that large and then install it. It would be much better to build a set of three cabinets, each 3' long. In fact, build one as a start, and then build the others as the need for more storage arises.

Make paper cutouts of generic rectangular shapes to represent potential storage units. If the storage is wall-mounted above another unit or apparatus, color the elements different colors so that they are visually separated.

Storage Options
- floor to ceiling
- wall-mounted above machines or benches
- under stairs
- under machines

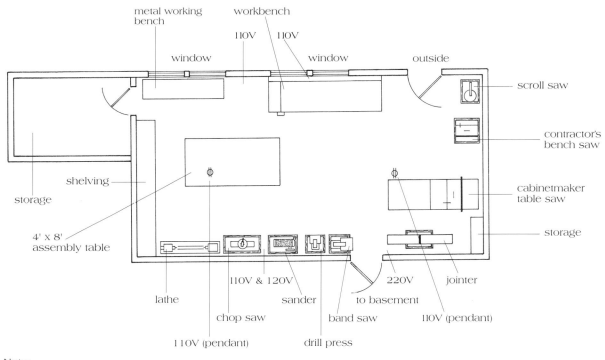

metal working bench

workbench

110V   110V

window   window   outside

scroll saw

contractor's bench saw

cabinetmaker table saw

shelving

storage

storage

4' x 8' assembly table

lathe

110V & 120V

sander

220V

jointer

to basement

band saw

110V (pendant)

110V (pendant)

drill press

Note:
All stationary machines
(except lathe) are on casters

George Levin's workshop

■ flush fit between wall studs
■ overhead in rafters

PLANNING MACHINE LOCATION

Two general rules apply to the location of the major machines—table saw, radial arm saw, jointer, planer and band saw—in the shop. First, certain machines, like the jointer and radial arm saw, are only used from one side. Second, there has to be enough room around other machines, such as the table saw and planer, for wood to enter and exit the machine. When using the paper cutouts, a logical starting point is to place the one-side-only machines against walls. Optionally, certain machines can be grouped together, such as placing the jointer and planer side by side. But make sure to allow enough space for long boards to safely clear a machine without bumping into other workshop items. For example, if a heavy board, 2″×8″×80″ is processed on a jointer, the operator not only has to maintain the board on the machine, but also has to be able to take the board from the out-feed table and not ram it against other workshop items. In other words, the entry and exit areas around certain machines must be clear: This space is as important as the space the machine occupies.

Table Saw

If full sheets of plywood are routinely cut, place the saw centrally in the workshop and build secondary support tables for the table saw. Remember to keep the pathway to and from the table saw unobstructed, so that the plywood can be safely handled and moved. For small workshops, panel saws are often used as an alternative to the table saw. These are wall-mounted

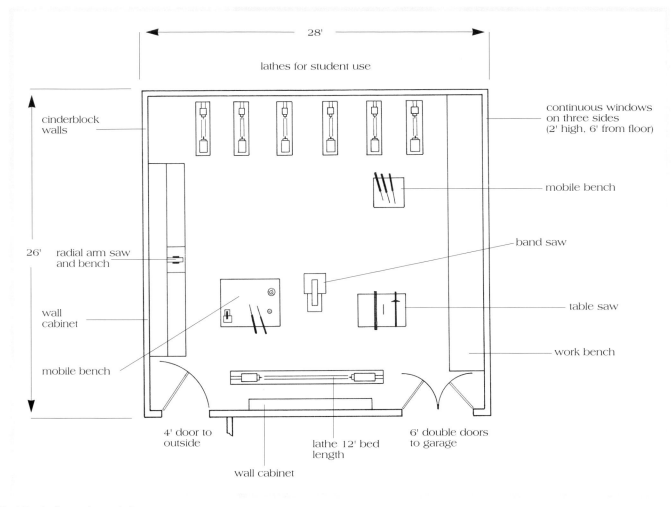

28'

lathes for student use

cinderblock
walls

continuous windows
on three sides
(2' high, 6' from floor)

mobile bench

band saw

26'   radial arm saw
       and bench

table saw

wall
cabinet

work bench

mobile bench

4' door to
outside

6' double doors
to garage

lathe 12' bed
length

wall cabinet

Ted Bartholomew's workshop

units that support the plywood, with a track-mounted circular saw for making the cuts.

Radial Arm Saw

If long boards are routinely cut with a radial saw, the saw should be placed against a wall, with long secondary support tables on either side of the saw. Many woodworkers with basement workshops set up a radial arm saw in the garage and perform rough cuts there, and then move the shorter pieces to the work-shop. **Note:** If the radial arm saw is in the garage and away from the main workshop, it should be equipped with a lock of some sort on the on/off switch. This prevents children or other curious types from turning on the saw when the owner isn't present.

Band Saw

If the band saw is used primarily for ripping and re-sawing long boards, it too can be located against a wall. This use requires a clear pathway for board entry and exit from the blade. However, if the band saw is used to make curved cuts, the board is moved in a radius manner, much like a clock hand, with the blade at the center point. For this type of use, the band saw should be more centered in the workshop, away from walls.

Dust Collector

The dust collector, although very useful, has to be one of the most difficult machines to place in the

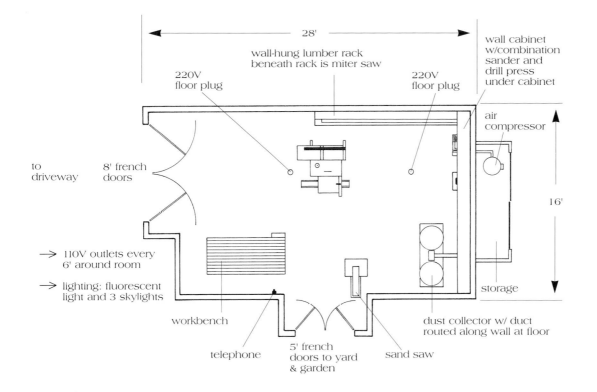

Charles Caswell's workshop

workshop. Not only is it dusty, but it's also very loud. (Personally, I'm hoping that someone will manufacture a dust collector that is quieter than a jet engine.) The other complication is ductwork, gates and connectors. To avoid having multiple ducts or hoses, the collector can be rolled next to a machine and used with a short section of hose. But this method only works if you're not doing much work and the floor is free of obstructions. A better method is to place the dust collector somewhere away from the work area and use ducts to the machines.

To control the dust that set-

tles around a collector and reduce the noise level, the dust collector can be located in a closet or small room. If you choose to do this, be certain that there is air flow into the room. Cut a square hole in the door and cover it with a furnace filter. The filter keeps dust from exiting the room, and the hole will reduce air pressure within the room. I've seen a dust collector room that, when the collector was running, created such air pressure that the door couldn't be opened. That isn't wise.

A number of machines are used primarily to process shorter lengths of wood. This allows for some freedom in floor plan use.

The drill press, router table, shaper, scroll saw and joinery machines can be located in less open areas. Occasionally, the router table or shaper is used for longer pieces; the machines can be moved for these specific operations.

PLAN FOR ELECTRICAL AND PLUMBING NEEDS

When a new building is under construction, there is a sequence to the order of events. That is, electricians and plumbers complete their work before drywallers and painters. While this sequence should apply when converting a basement or garage

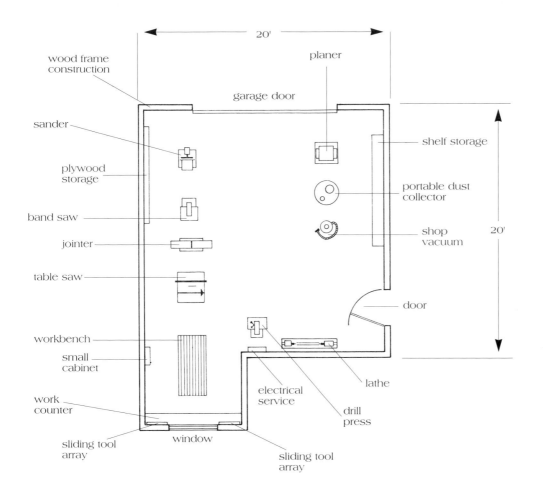

wood frame construction

planer

garage door

20'

sander

plywood storage

band saw

jointer

table saw

workbench

small cabinet

work counter

sliding tool array

window

electrical service

drill press

lathe

shelf storage

portable dust collector

shop vacuum

door

20'

sliding tool array

David Beyl's workshop

into a woodshop, the electrical wiring and plumbing are often overlooked. The one or two existing outlets in the garage or basement are "upgraded" by the use of extension cords and extension bars. And if there is a laundry sink or toilet already in the garage or basement, it is left as is. Wouldn't it seem to be much smarter to upgrade both the electrical systems and plumbing while designing the workshop?

Wiring the Shop

The importance of having a proper electrical service cannot be overstated. First, I advise against using very long extension cords. Not only do they create more floor clutter, but long extension cords can lead to unnecessary electrical motor wear. A representative from an air compressor company once told me that the majority of compressors returned for motor repairs were those that were used with extension cords. Apparently, the owners forgot that longer air hoses are a better way to work at a distance from the compressor. I have one retract-

able ceiling-mounted extension cord in my workshop. It's 30' long 14/3 SJT wire and rated at 13A, 125V, 1625 watts. I only use it with hand drills, finish sanders and similar tools. I would never use it for band saws and other stationary machines.

The placement of machines relative to the proper outlet is fundamental. If you want to use the table saw at a particular location, having an isolated 110V or 220V outlet at that location is mandatory. Since this section is about guidelines for designing the workshop, the key factors are wiring from an existing service panel (interior or exterior to the wall), installing a subpanel, outlet locations and location of lights.

Interior wiring is difficult when the wall studs and ceiling rafters are already covered. Exterior wiring through conduits is a primary option, especially when adding wires and circuits. If the framework is still open, it's straightforward to run wiring through the studs, around windows and door frames to the service. Subpanels are a very good choice when upgrading the workshop. They are easily mounted near the main service panel, and conduit can then be routed anywhere in the workshop.

The design of the outlets should accommodate both the placement of machines and the use of electrical tools at various locations. There should be outlets near both ends and at the center of the workbench, as well as outlets near the open areas in the workshop that can be used for assembly and detail work. For example, you have constructed a 3'-wide, 7'-high bookcase and want to use a router for detail work on its sides. If the bookcase is set on the workbench, it may be too high up for safe and easy work. If the bookcase is on the floor in an assembly area, the

work height is correct. An overhead outlet or outlet about three feet from the floor will facilitate the router's use.

Shop Plumbing Concerns

The same generalities apply to plumbing: Is plumbing necessary in a workshop? From a design viewpoint, if form and function are considered, the question is, "What value does plumbing serve?" What I value in a workshop sink, besides washing my hands, is that it permits me to maintain waterstones for sharpening, mix dyes and water-soluble finishes, clean the HVLP spray gun and nozzle, clean restoration projects and use the new polyurethane glues. If there is a sink in the workshop, don't use it to pour away toxic solvents and other hazardous wastes. Water, soap, dirt and grime are the only things that should go down the drain.

Garage and basement workshops are often near laundry rooms. This proximity permits the addition of new water pipes to the workshop area. Copper and PVC pipes are fairly easy to work with, and it shouldn't be too complicated to route pipes several feet to the workshop. If you aren't sure about cutting into water pipes, call a plumbing contractor for assistance. Undoubtedly, he can do the work

faster than a woodworker!

Once the electrical system and plumbing needs have been determined, add these elements to the master plan and draw them onto the planning grid. Hopefully, the proposed workshop design will accommodate all of these elements.

SUMMARIZING THE DESIGNING OF A WORKSHOP

1. Create a master plan of all the key workshop elements: machines, tools, workbench, open areas, lumber racks, storage, electrical and plumbing.

2. Be realistic, as much as possible, and know your own personal interests.

3. Be somewhat hypothetical in choosing the workshop elements. At this point you haven't spent any money.

4. Make paper mock-ups of different workshop layouts.

5. Be reasonable. Understand that a workshop takes time and money to create, and that you can proceed at your own pace of acquisition.

6. Always consider alternatives. Buy inexpensive, resell and buy more expensive. Consider multipurpose machines. Consider hand tools instead of power tools.

5

EXAMINING WORKSHOP EXAMPLES

It's very difficult to find representative workshops that reveal all the mysteries of setting up a workshop. Each of the shops that I have visited is unique and represents the owner's personality and woodworking style. The quest for the perfect workshop really begins and ends with each person's own effort. And, while it's enjoyable to peek into another woodshop, often the only transferable items are bits and pieces of problem solving. We seem to have a collective desire to construct "model cities," "dream houses" and "ideal workshops," but the reality is that these places are curiosities. Anyone remember the futuristic cities of the 1939 New York World's Fair, Disneyland's House of the Future or General Electric's 1960s All-Electric House? The point is, while we idealize a perfect workshop, *your* perfect workshop is right in front of you—it's in the garage, the basement, the extra room, the attic or a closet. All you need to do is get started.

The following perspective is from Alan Boardman, a very talented woodworker and authentic expert on tools, joinery and wood. I attended his lectures on joinery and tuning up hand tools about 20 years ago, and he showed me the fantastic enchantment of woodworking. I now prize the small (small-marble-size) wooden puzzles he makes. "Regarding the ideal workshop, if one exists, I'll bet it is owned by someone who does no woodworking whatsoever. My shop is a total disgrace and I love it. Every minute I spend wondering how to make it closer to ideal is a minute I am not enjoying working in it. My wife calls it my hellhole. It is a jumble of offcuts and boxes that I have long ago stopped wondering the contents of. I can hardly move about in the place or swing a board or find a precious piece of rare wood I have been saving for decades for that worthy project, yet I am always happy there and never think of food or aging pains. If others think like I do, maybe the ideal shop is better described in human terms than where every machine should be placed and how to store odd nuts and bolts. Incidentally, I haven't always felt this way: I used to dream of a perfect shop. But now that I am retired and theoretically have the time to redo it, I find that I don't want to. I like it the way it is."

The following workshops can be classified into three types: the garage and basement workshop, the separate-building workshop on the home property and the rental-space workshop. These example workshops have been in existence for some time, and each of them definitely reflects the personality and style of the owner.

GARAGE AND BASEMENT WORKSHOPS

Mark Kulseth's Workshop

Mark Kulseth has been using his workshop for about five years. His workshop is in a single-car garage and the adjacent laundry and storage areas in a 64-year-old house. His workshop measures 20′×28′ (560 square feet). It is wired from the main house electrical service for both 110V and 220V use. Additionally, some areas of the workshop have a floor-to-ceiling height of 6′ 5″. Mark is a part-time professional whose main woodworking interests are making custom furniture and some repairs and restorations. He also collects antique tools.

While there is little free space in Mark's workshop, he has maximized the existing floor and wall areas so well that he can build standard-size cabinets and furniture.

His principal machinery (in order of importance) includes:

- 10″ Delta Unisaw with 52″ fence and outfeed table
- 14″ Delta band saw with riser block
- 20″ Jet drill press
- Delta 6″×48″ belt sander
- 12″ disc sanding machine
- Jet 1200 CFM dust collector
- Walker-Turner lathe
- traditionally designed workbench

If Mark had more floor space, he would add a wide-belt sanding machine, a downdraft sanding table and a five-foot-square work surface that is accessible from all four sides.

There are several nifty features to Mark's workshop: He has grouped benches and tools around the furnace and chimney, has displayed plumb bobs from under the stairs, has a hidden storage area for lumber and combined built-in bench tops/cabinet storage and shelves for antique tools. When I first visited his workshop, I was taken with how Mark has stored tools and stuff in every conceivable location—between rafters, behind walls and suspended in corners. My thought was that if he ever moved to another workshop, he would need significant cabinet storage to handle all of the tucked-away items hidden in his workshop. He should also use a metal detector to be certain that nothing is left behind!

Safety is important in Mark's work. He says that he has learned from the mistakes of others and he always wears eye and hearing protection. There is a first-aid box and three fire extinguishers in the workshop. Also, flammable and combustible materials are kept in a metal locker. Rags are rinsed in water, air-dried and then placed in a small metal garbage can inside the workshop.

I believe that woodworkers, such as Mark, who work in confined areas often develop a keen sense of what might be better for more ideal working conditions. Mark states that if he could design his ideal workshop, he

Kulseth's workshop and more countertop and shelving for antique tools.

Mark Kulseth uses the underside of stairs to display his plumb bob collection.

The Kulseth workshop crawl space (hidden behind the chart) is actually a large area for storing lumber.

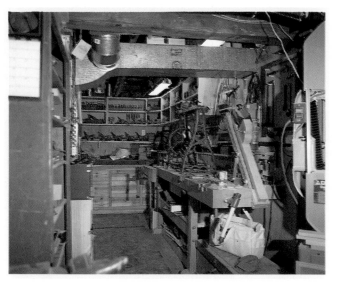

Mark Kulseth stores his antique plane collection above his workbench. An angled hold-down device is in the foreground.

Mark Kulseth has an older home with a single-car garage attached to the laundry room and storage area. The table saw is located near the back wall of the garage.

Kulseth's workshop with countertop area and shelf storage. Mark plans on installing cabinet doors in the near future. Note that the spindle sander sits on the box that houses the air compressor.

would have "a workshop with ample space, wood floors, tall ceilings and maybe a separate finishing room and office, free of dust. But more than anything, I would love a shop built in a natural setting, away from the city, with mountain views, trees, a river and so on. To do this, I must have the business demands for my products."

Mark does see a relationship between himself, his workshop and his woodworking skills. He says, "I try to make my shop reflect my personality and skills as a craftsman. If I'm making a tool rack, I make it with care and pride to show my skills. It makes it much more enjoyable to view my tools. I also collect antique tools and many are displayed in my work area. I often reflect on the craftsmen of old while trying to solve my building problems. This reflection seems to inspire a higher quality in my craft."

David Beyl's Workshop

The David Beyl workshop was a two-car garage. The house is 27 years old, and David has had the workshop for 13 years. The workshop measures 20'×20', with an 8' ceiling. It has a sub-panel with both 110V and 220V wiring. David is a part-time professional who specializes in building furniture, repairing antiques and teaching woodworking. He spends about 20 hours a week in the workshop.

His principal machinery (in order of importance) includes:

- 10" Delta Cabinetmaker's saw
- 6" Jet jointer
- 14" Delta bandsaw
- 12" disc/6"×48" belt sander
- 16" Delta radial drill press
- 12' Shopsmith planer
- Shopsmith dust collector
- 14" Delta scroll saw
- Campbell/Hausfield air compressor
- 12" Delta lathe

David's workshop is 20'×20'; that is, a square floor pattern with almost no nooks and crannies. Interestingly, David's concept of woodworking seems to match the straightforward workshop layout: He's somewhat of a minimalist and only has tools and machines that he uses. Nothing more, nothing less. The simplicity of the workshop also lends itself to teaching woodworking. Students aren't working in clutter, and they *are* learning to use the basic machinery in a clean and straightforward workshop environment.

Just because David has identified his woodworking style and workshop arrangement doesn't mean that he wouldn't improve his workshop. If he remodeled the workshop, he would include a built-in dust collection system, recessed lighting (fluorescent and incandescent), a sink with hot water, a gas heating system, a separate office area, convenient storage and a modern-design workbench.

A feature that I particularly admired is David's use of sliding tool storage partitions. These partitions are four panels that slide like sliding closet doors, except the units are wall-mounted and slide back and forth in front of a window. Slender tools such as chisels, screwdrivers, pliers and files are stored on the racks.

George Levin's Workshop

The George Levin workshop is located at basement level with a window view and door access to the outside. The workshop is approximately 14'×29', has a

David Beyl has a two-car-garage workshop. To maximize space, numerous sliding panels are mounted in front of windows.

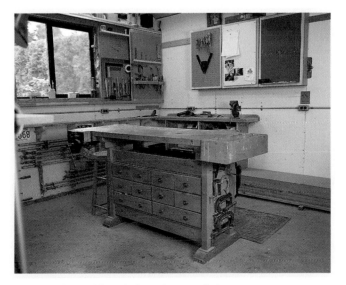

David Beyl's workbench featuring small drawers.

David Beyl has small cabinets that have pagelike sections for holding small tools.

The David Beyl workshop has wood storage units that are hinged at one end and then roll out at the other end. This storage unit is used primarily for plywood and cutoff pieces of plywood.

George Levin's workbench and window view.

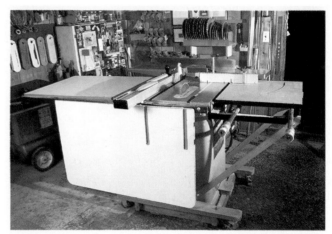

George Levin's table saw is mounted on a shop-made mobile base.

standard-height ceiling and is equipped with 110V and 220V electrical wiring. The house is 71 years old, and George has been using the workshop for 22 years. He considers himself to be a part-time professional and builds Federal and Deco style furniture and other built-ins. He spends about 20 hours a week in the workshop.

His principal machinery (in order of importance) includes:
- 10" Delta Unisaw
- 10" Inca Model 510 jointer/planer
- 8" Grizzly jointer
- 14" Powermatic band saw
- 10" disc/6" belt Delta sander
- 24" Delta scroll saw
- 6"×32" Delta (Homecraft) lathe

If there were space in the workshop, George would have a panel saw. Also, if he could design an ideal workshop, he would include a spray booth, large doors, plenty of windows, level access to the outside, wood flooring, a sink and a toilet, a dust collection system, room for wood and sheet goods storage.

George's workshop is an

elongated rectangle, and he has optimized working conditions within the space by making mobile bases for the machines. These bases are made of wood,

A heavy belt sander is also mounted on shop-made mobile base. Note customized sander fence.

George Levin designed his workbench holding system, which features a slot perpendicular to the vise. The slot contains movable and lockable bench dog.

with locking wheels, and they are both sturdy and easy to use. It is easy to roll the table saw into a more open position, use it and then return it. Another principal feature is a 4′ × 8′ assembly table. This table is about 24″ high, and the top is a sheet of ¾″ melamine particleboard. The table is used for stacking rough-cut pieces, for assembly and gluing of workpieces and for finishing work. When the top surface is no longer workable, it is flipped over to access the other side. And when both sides are worn out, a new piece is installed and the old top is disposed of.

George has a spectacular workbench. Its wonderfully unique construction is a fine example of craftsmanship and represents an impressive comprehension of design. The workbench measures about 3′ × 12′, and it is mounted against a wall. Looking at the front, the right-side half is composed of two rows of drawers that have customized pockets for hand tools; the left side is an open area, usually filled with large sleeping dogs. There is only one metal vise, mounted on the left-front edge, and it has an adjustable companion holder (workpiece support) that can be located on any of the four vertical bench supports. Instead of the typical bench dogs (I don't mean the ones asleep under the

bench), the bench top has a metal track perpendicular to the vise. An adjustable stop slides in the track so that various widths of board can be easily secured. Other details include a small tool tray located along the entire back edge, and the top surface material is hardboard. When the hardboard wears out, it is unscrewed, removed and then replaced with new hardboard.

George has a sense of humor, and his workshop reflects his personal view of things. In a way, his workshop is a collage of bits and pieces of personal history, world events, successes of children and just fun stuff. A plain storage cabinet is totally covered with tiny pictures of dogs and, although the cabinet contains nuts and bolts, it's referred to as the "dog cabinet." George once was an avid aviator, and so it stands to reason that the ceiling is covered with pictures of airplanes and an upside-down remote control airplane! Where most of us have machines with the manufacturer's name prominently displayed, George has covered his band saw with vacation pictures, quotes and other less commercial concepts. There are numerous calendars from the 1960s, posters of long-ago lectures, old clocks and assorted keepsakes—enough interesting things to keep a smile on anyone's face. Judging by the

George Levin's workshop is about the size of a one-car garage. He has a beautifully designed workbench mounted against the wall.

The Levin bench has drawers with custom locations for all tools.

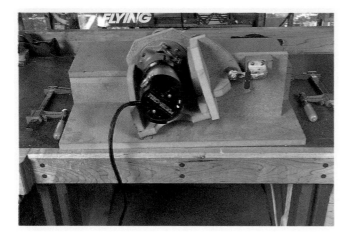

Because the Levin workshop is small, George has many jigs and fixtures that he uses at the workbench. Shown is a mortising jig.

Exterior of Charles Caswell's workshop. Note that double French doors are located where the garage door is normally located.

workshop, George Levin is a happy man. He comments about his workshop: "This room is an extension of myself, so it contains pictures and memorabilia reflecting some of my other interests so that I really feel 'at home' when I am working there."

SEPARATE-BUILDING OR SEPARATE-ROOM WORKSHOPS

This category is represented by two different styles: a workshop that looks like a stand-alone garage but isn't, and a workshop that was built attached to a house. Both of these workshops came into existence because of the owner's specific interests and need for space.

Charles Caswell's Workshop

After years of working in other people's workshops, Charles decided to build his ideal workshop. His goal was to design a workshop that would be on his own property and separate from the house. His house property's shape is that of a typical city lot; that is, a long and narrow rectangle. The house is an older style with the garage as a separate structure, back from the house and next to the property line. Charles removed the old garage and then designed the workshop to look like a new garage. The exterior is reminiscent of the bungalow style, with door overhangs and clapboard siding. The major

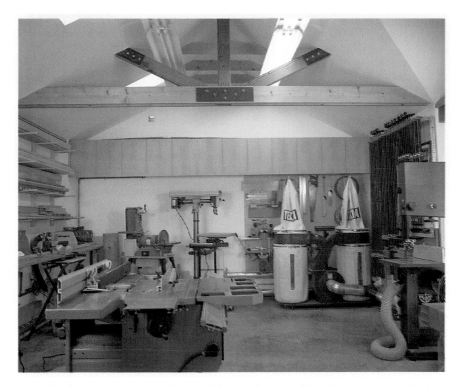

Caswell built a two-car-garage size workshop at the end of his driveway on a typical city lot. This interior view shows the open ceiling, skylights, lighting, main storage cabinets and machinery. Not seen, to the right side, is a traditional workbench. Charles is a furniture maker who believes in simplicity, neatness and cleanliness, and his model workshop is noteworthy for both its straightforward layout and its comfortable work conditions.

View of clamp storage in the Caswell workshop.

der of importance) includes:

- 10″ Robland X31 table saw with sliding table
- Robland X31 jointer/planer combination machine
- 18″ Laguna band saw
- Ryobi miter saw
- AMC radial head drill press
- Robland X31 shaper
- Robland X31 horizontal mortiser
- Grizzly belt/disc combination sander

exterior feature, which reveals something of the nature of the building, is that Charles installed French doors instead of a garage door. Charles also built the walls with sound insulation so that the neighbors wouldn't be hearing machinery noise. From my own experiences visiting the workshop, I had to be fairly close to it to hear the muffled sounds of a dust collector and planer being used. His soundproofing consisted of using standard wall insulation between wall studs and then covering that with ½″ sound board ("sound stop"). Drywall

board was installed in the normal fashion and the wall was finished and painted.

Charles is a full-time professional woodworker and spends over 50 hours a week in the workshop building furniture. His workshop is two years old, has 450 square feet and 110V and 220V wiring. There are electrical outlets at convenient wall locations and 220V floor plugs near the table saw. This outlet eliminates having an AC cord from the machine to the wall, thus reducing tripping hazards.

His principal machinery (in or-

Charles also has a 4-bag dust collector in the workshop, but he thinks that the hook-up at the machines is inadequate; that is, the factory-constructed fittings are ineffective at the source of dust. He would rather have a larger, more powerful unit, including a chip separator, located in a separate space. After the photographs of his workshop were taken, he replaced the upper filter bags with larger bags that filter dust at the 5 micron level. This has considerably reduced dust blowback into the work area.

Charles also has a 6 hp, 80

Ted Bartholomew has a workshop attached to a two-car garage. Windows are continuous on three sides of workshop.

Ted Bartholomew's custom lathe is designed for working on either side of the machine. The portable tool storage cart is easily moved throughout the workshop.

doesn't consider this to be a principal tool because he uses it mostly for cleanup work. He bought the large compressor partly for value and partly because it's quieter than the smaller "oil-less" compressors. Under normal usage, it cycles on a few times a week.

The workshop features a very comfortable, bright and airy working area with an open ceiling, skylights and one 5'-wide and one 8'-wide French doors. For storage, Charles built a single row of cabinets across the back wall. These cabinets are located at approximately head height and are the only storage in the workshop. There is also a wall section with pegboard that is used for oversize tools and accessories. There is lumber storage, positioned above the miter saw area, which is used for planed boards and material be-

ing prepared for the next work project.

The workshop reflects Charles' attitude about woodworking: It is thoughtful, organized and well crafted. He has enough tools and machinery for any work, and the room is clean and open so there's no inefficiency due to clutter and congestion. He is very content with his workshop and would only add a warehouse area for curing and storing lumber.

Ted Bartholomew's Workshop

The Ted Bartholomew workshop is one of the most unusual workshops I've visited. Ted's workshop measures 26' × 28' (728 square feet) with a 9' ceiling. There is both 110V and 220V wiring. The room, built as a workshop 20 years ago, is located next to the garage. The most no-

ticeable feature of the room is that there are windows, located 6' from the floor, continuous on three walls. These windows are 2' high, and the lighting is similar to that of skylighting. What makes the workshop unique is that Ted is a "serious amateur" who specializes in wood turning: He likes turning large bowls, he teaches wood turning and he manufactures his own wood lathe.

There are large and small movable tables and carts for storing lathe tools and accessories. His lathe features a pneumatic forward and reversing system so turning work can be done on either side of the lathe. In order to make it easy to access lathe tools, the tools are simply laid on a cart, and the cart is moved to the area of work. These movable tables and carts also make it easier to work when several students are working at the lathes.

His principal machinery (in order of importance) includes:

- lathes
- several Bartholomew lathes (the number varies)
- antique lathe—4 hp, capacity of 22" overbed, 7' outboard, 12' overall
- Walker-Turner 16" band saw
- Craftsman 10" radial arm saw
- 10" Delta Unisaw
- Drill press
- 1" belt sander

RENTAL-SPACE WORKSHOPS

Dean Bershaw's Workshop

Dean Bershaw is a full-time professional woodworker specializing in contemporary furniture. He has been in his current workshop 3½ years and spends 30 to 50 hours a week there. He rents part of the basement in a commercial building that was built in the 1950s. His workshop measures 50'×20' (1000 square feet) with a ceiling height of 7' 8" under the ceiling beams and 9' between the beams. There is both 110V and 220V wiring.

His principle machinery includes (in order of importance):

- 10" Jet 3 hp table saw
- 6" Grizzly jointer
- 12" Delta planer
- 10" Delta radial arm saw
- 9" Grizzly disc sander
- Mark 1 drill press
- 2 hp Grizzly dust collector
- Router table with Porter Cable router, Incra Jig fence
- 24" Windmaster fan
- 6 hp, 30 gal. Campbell-Hausfield air compressor
- 4"×132" Delta belt sander
- 12" Delta lathe
- Star oscillating spindle sander
- Delta sharpening center

Having a commercial operation in a concrete basement offers several challenges worth noting.

Basements in industrial/commercial areas aren't necessarily the easiest locations to find. Both vendors and customers require clear instructions in order to find Dean's workshop. Although Dean doesn't expect walk-in business, he does have new designers and buyers who want to visit him while projects are under construction. Other basement complications include no direct access to the outside, risk of water damage (broken/leaking pipes) and ventilation difficulties.

Dean's workshop is in the back section of the building's basement; consequently, there are no windows, doors or other vents to the outside. However, at one time there was an opening in a wall, which was later bricked in when another building was built next to that wall. Dean removed the bricks and discovered that there is a 5"-wide space between the buildings. He built

Dean Bershaw has four workstations with surfaces of 4'×8' sheets of particleboard.

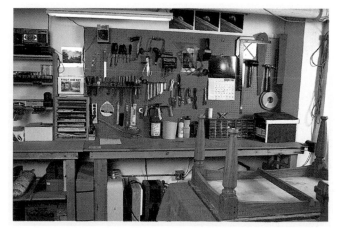

The Dean Bershaw workshop is located in the basement of a commercial building. Note the area for smaller work projects and tool storage.

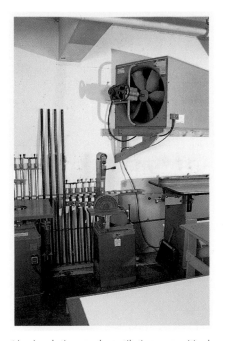

Air circulation and ventilation are critical in the basement workshop. The only access directly to the outside was an opening to a 5″ space between building walls. Dean Bershaw built a diagonally mounted fan housing so that air could be exhausted into the narrow space between buildings.

an angled exhaust fan housing and installed it in front of the opening. This clever arrangement exhausts stale workshop air into the 5″ space. This fan, although it does remove residual dust particles, is not meant to be a dust collector system—it is used to refresh and circulate air in the workshop. And, there are no windows on either of the walls at higher locations (i.e., no one will be bothered by exhausted workshop air).

Although water leakage is always a worry, it has yet to happen. Preparing for such a problem, Dean has made all storage units, tables and workstations as

modular units so they are easy to move.

If Dean remodeled his workshop, he would add a spray booth, office space and living quarters. He would include space for multi-use capabilities, such as automotive work and metalwork, and would also add windows, higher ceilings and openings at opposite ends of the workshop for through-circulation.

The principal factor that makes this location attractive is the rental rate. The rent is affordable, allowing him to keep his operating costs low. He is willing to compromise with ceiling height and no windows in order to be competitive. Dean realizes that time is of the essence when doing custom work. Any workshop improvements have to serve a purpose and not require significant amounts of time to accomplish. Dean also states: "I have bought tools for a specific job but they all have subsequent value for general-usage applications. In my view, the less specific the application, the better."

ANOTHER APPROACH
James Leary's Workplace
James, a successful woodworker, does mostly house remodeling and refurbishing—and he doesn't have a workshop. Instead, he takes his workplace with him to the job site. His large

van holds all that he needs; he simply drives up and begins to work. He says that he made a design choice: He could have built custom storage within the van, but decided not to. Instead, he decided to use tool cases that are specific for each power tool. His reasoning was that fixed storage is somewhat limiting. For example, if a job requires drills and reciprocating saws, but not routers and power washers, he can leave the unnecessary equipment at home. Also, the tool cases all have shapes and sizes that are easily identified for quick selection while working. And modern tool cases are easy to carry, are reasonably dustproof and water resistant and hold extra bits, blades and accessories. There is one other bonus: Customers enjoy and appreciate his readiness and thoroughness.

APPLY TO YOUR OWN SHOP
I have visited dozens of workshops, and they all have the basic assortment of tools, storage and such. Does having a particular brand of tools make the workshop better? No. Does having a large space make woodworking better? Perhaps. Does personal problem solving help make an ideal workshop? Yes.

Although a woodcarver or someone working on small-scale projects doesn't necessarily re-

Jim Leary doesn't have a typical workshop—his workshop is his van. He does remodeling and general woodworking, and drives his workshop to the work site.

Almost everything is out of Jim's van.

quire large areas for work, the general-purpose woodworker does benefit from having adequate space. Unfortunately, if you have 100 square feet of workshop, you can't simply wish up another 50 square feet to make the room better. What you can do is

- wisely plan out the space.
- buy appropriately sized machines.

- have only the machines and tools that you need.
- build storage units to fit the space.
- be happy and build things.

Even if you have more space than necessary (which hardly ever occurs), the same basic steps apply.

Each of the workshops I have profiled is a consequence of these basic steps. All of the

woodworkers have adapted to the room configuration, organized the machinery and storage around their needs, and then proceeded to make furniture, turn bowls, repair antiques, collect old tools, remodel houses and lose themselves in the enjoyment, wonder and mystery of woodworking.

6

CREATING USEFUL STORAGE SPACE

■

Storage units have a curious nature: They must provide sheltered organization for most workshop items, yet they shouldn't take up too much valuable room space.

WHY STORE STUFF AT ALL?

I've never been certain about the concept behind the need for storage space. Do we store things for organizational reasons, clutter control, easy access or because we have too much stuff? Ideally, any part, accessory or tool should be within reach during the work process. Realistically, however, everyone has shelves, cabinets, drawers, walls, hangers, rafters, bins, boxes, barrels, racks and trunks full of the useful, rare, odd and ordinary. We usually have favorite tools stored individually at arm's length, and ev-

erything else is put away. Diet books and storage books have something in common—sheer numbers. There are hundreds of books, magazines and videos offering every conceivable solution to taming the flotsam and jetsam—or the delicate and valuable objects—of our lives. And one more point: Woodworkers make objects. We either make artistic objects or we make cabinets, shelves, drawers and boxes for storing and displaying everything and anything.

Woodworkers are collectors. We collect everything that seems useful, and we justify our collecting with the rationale that we need it—or *will* need it someday. It always sounds reasonable to say, "I need a complete set of brad-point drill bits, including $\frac{9}{64}$″ and $\frac{7}{32}$″. Realistically, you may only

need ¼″, ⅜″ and ½″ brad-point bits, but there's always the uncertainty that leads you to believe that a set of 12 bits is necessary. Besides, the tool catalogs state that having a set of 12 bits is useful.

Clamp storage in Bill Stankus's workshop. Upper beam has angled face so that clamps are suspended at an angle.

Three types of storage: cabinet storage for the drill press, pegboard storage for infrequently used accessories and workbench shelf storage.

age. If the room is built and the machines are in place, start by standing near each machine and imagining what work will be like, and what tools and accessories might be needed while working. Determine the needs for all machines and then make a master list for the entire workshop. An example list might include:

Table Saw

- 3 each saw blades
- tenon jig
- push sticks
- miter guide
- feather board
- angle fence
- dado set

Band Saw

- 5 each blades
- circle cutter
- miter guide
- fence

Planer

- dial indicator
- spare knives
- table wax

Drill Press

- drill index
- multispur bits
- sanding drum set
- extra-length bits

Besides collecting extras of any given object, woodworkers also collect interesting tools, wood, information (books, magazines and plans), accessories, gadgets and finishing products. We generally obtain these items as if space and storage aren't of any concern. We don't just have one of anything; we like sets and collections so much that we go on quests to complete a particular set. We specialize in our tools and things so much that we become experts on the rare and unusual. We join clubs devoted to antique tools or wood samples. We track down obscure and out-of-the-way dealers in order to possess hard-to-find Stanley Bedrock planes or pieces of Pink Ivory. No one

should doubt that woodworkers are at the center of the storage issue as both creators and users.

TYPES OF WORKSHOP STORAGE

- Floor-level and wall-hung cabinets
- Modular, free-standing cabinets
- Portable units
- Shelving
- Pegboard
- Lumber storage

ORGANIZE SHOP STORAGE

After you have established the locations of machines and the workbench within the woodshop space, it's time to organize stor-

Consider Your Options

Once the list is completed, consider storage options: shelves, open wall hangers, open

Inside of drill press storage cabinet.

cabinets, closed cabinets, drawers and so on. Then ask yourself, Is one or more storage units necessary? Is there a need for one local storage center, or does each machine need its own storage? Note those tools, such as a dial indicator, that should be kept dust-free and those tools unaffected by dust (band saw blades). Also, drill bits are easily lost in clutter; they are best kept in orderly sets.

DESIGNING STORAGE SPACE

The next planning step is extremely critical to the overall workshop plan. Basically, two very different designs can be selected, and each will fundamentally affect the workshop. The choice is that of having randomly designed storage or having unified storage.

Random Storage

Random storage is characterized by what is generally done: a hodgepodge of shelves, pegboard, hooks and cabinets. *Unified storage* is exemplified by similarly designed cabinets, usually found in kitchens, baths and design books. Most workshops have random storage because new things are added over long periods of time. Interestingly, hodgepodge storage doesn't mean that things can't be found. After awhile, most woodworkers know where they stored the no. 8 brass roundhead screws. It all becomes second nature.

Unified Storage

Unified workshop storage should, at its best, maximize the available space or area allotted for storage. This can be accomplished by designing storage units so that there are no *dead* areas. For example, instead of a 5'-high cabinet, make it floor-to-ceiling and use the upper shelves for infrequently used items. Or construct European-style cabinets because they have less wasted internal space. Avoid using cabinets and boxes simply because you have them.

MATERIALS AND STORAGE DESIGN

The design of storage units will be influenced by the type of materials used. Solid-wood construction procedures will be different than those needed for working man-made materials.

Solid Wood Construction

If solid wood constructions are desired, a number of woodworking tools and skills are required. For example, suppose you want to build a Shaker-style wall cabinet. The following are the generalized steps needed to duplicate or simulate this early-1800s construction:

1. Purchase rough lumber approximately 1" to 1½" in thickness. Allow for waste and order 20–30% more than the project requires. Typical woods are pine, cherry and oak.

2. Plane lumber to different thicknesses, varying from ⅝" to 1".

3. Use a hand plane or joiner to square and straighten edges.

4. Glue boards edge-to-edge to make wider pieces.

5. Construct the basic cabinet box using joinery: traditional dovetails or modern joints, such as box joints, plate joinery, dowels or screws.

6. Construct internal framework consisting of different sizes of wood. Use hand tools, and use the router to make rabbets and sliding dovetail-type joints.

7. Construct frame-and-panel doors consisting of tongue-

and-groove and mortise-and-tenon joinery. Use chisels, a saw, hand planes and a router table or shaper.

8. Construct drawers with dovetail joints. Use hand tools, a router and a dovetail jig.

9. Fit doors and drawers to cabinet so that seasonal weather changes won't cause them to stick, bind or be too loose fitting.

Using Man-Made Materials

In contrast, the construction of a modern cabinet using man-made materials follows a different series of steps.

1. Purchase ½"- and ¾"-thick materials. Itemize cutting list and purchase necessary amount of materials. Typical materials are particleboard and medium-density fiberboard (MDF).

2. Cut materials to size.

3. Assemble materials with butt or rabbet joints. Use a router, plate joinery, screws and nails.

4. Cover exposed edges with veneer-type tape or strips of solid wood.

5. Use either face-frame or the frameless European cabinet construction for the front of cabinet.

6. Construct drawers with dadoes and grooves. Use the router, and screws or nails.

CABINET CONSTRUCTION

Most modern cabinet constructions use a blend of man-made materials and solid wood. It's common to see cabinets that have plywood sides, top, bottom, and shelves, and solid-wood doors, door frame and drawer fronts.

Face-Frame Cabinets

Typically, the face-frame cabinet has a 2"-wide frame covering the front edge of the cabinet. The frame thus reduces the size of the cabinet opening, with doors and drawers smaller than the cabinet width. Doors are attached to the frame with exposed hinges; drawer fronts usually overlap onto the frame. The toe space at the cabinet's base is made by cutting notches into the side pieces.

European-Style Cabinets

The frameless, or European, cabinet has no face frame. Instead, the front edges are covered to the same width as the cabinet box material thickness. Doors and drawers are usually flush to the cabinet edges and each other. That means more usable interior space. European cabinets are sometimes referred to as "the 32 millimeter system" because of the standardization of using 32 millimeters as the space between hinge fittings, shelf-support holes and cabinet joints. Frameless cabinets are generally

made as a box and then attached to a separate base frame. This allows for the toe space as well as different height bases.

DO IT YOURSELF OR NOT?

It's an old saying that woodworkers should build their own workshop cabinets and benches in order to understand, practice and refine various woodworking skills. While there is nothing wrong with this viewpoint, I would like to offer an update on this old saying by breaking it down into various elements, somewhat like a logic puzzle. Ponder the following thoughts and questions:

1. Building storage cabinets for the workshop is really preparation for using the workshop. The opposite of storage is having random piles of stuff.

2. If you are an amateur or hobby woodworker, how much time do you have to devote to woodworking?

3. Is cost-effectiveness an issue?

4. What machines and tools are available for building storage?

5. How will you transport materials?

6. Is the location for storage unusual, unique or average (i.e., the need for special or standard-size storage)?

7. What will you learn about woodworking by cutting

particleboard or drilling holes?

8. Can you make it the same as, or better than, commercial storage units?

9. Is the woodworking process (including making storage units) one of self-expression, personal enrichment and an element of quality of life?

Consider Time and Money

I'm not sure that it's easy to answer each of these questions with a simple response. However, a few parts are very real; that is, time and money. Very often it takes considerable time to design, purchase materials, build and install cabinets and other storage units. We may watch someone on TV build a cabinet during a 30 minute program, but I can assure you that real-life woodworking takes significantly longer. Ask yourself, "How much is my free time worth?"

BUILDING SHOP STORAGE

Basic storage units are shelves, wall hooks and hangers, bookcase-style open cabinets, racks and cabinets with shelves, drawers and doors. Wall-hung devices and shelves are inexpensive and easily installed; cabinets require more materials, construction skills and machinery. Very often simple shelving, hooks and hangers are used simply because of installation simplicity. Pegboard wall coverings offer

real storage value, and open shelving has serious limitations. The disadvantage of open shelving is that it is open; shelves unattached to wall hangers are easily unbalanced and subject to tipping when heavy tools are stored on them. Open shelving units are useless for storing items that you want dustfree; items should be sealed away in boxes when dustfree storage is required. And if there are several boxes on a shelf, detailed labeling is required; otherwise, it's difficult to locate items. Perhaps it's best to think of shelving as a bag of candy: It's OK to to have one or two pieces (a few shelves), but don't have a diet of it (not everywhere in your workshop).

Ideally, workshop storage should be based on cabinets and/or pegboard. Within these two storage types, worlds of possibilities exist. Furthermore, pegboard offers simple storage solutions; cabinets offer creative storage possibilities.

BUILDING EUROPEAN-STYLE CABINETS

I suggest that construction of efficient storage units begins with accepting the benefits of the European frameless cabinet design. Apart from the European design, first consider the kinds of building materials.

Choosing Materials

Georgia-Pacific is one of the larger manufacturers of man-made materials, and they

Built-in workbench with open storage area. Plastic containers are used for holding odds and ends.

Tall cabinet holds accessories near the workbench. Cabinet features angled shelf for easy access to hand planes.

Pegboard storage.

Open cabinet for frequently used power tools.

broadly classify the common materials into "engineered board and structural panels." Particleboard, medium-density fiberboard (MDF) and hardboard are termed *engineered board*; plywood and oriented strand board (OSB) are *structural panels*. Structural panels are used primarily for house construction. Quality grades of particleboard, MDF and hardboard make ideal cabinet materials if they are used properly. They are readily available, cost less than solid wood or plywood and have dimensional stability, flatness and no voids.

EVALUATING MAN-MADE MATERIALS The disadvantages of particleboard must also be considered. First, particleboard is made with urea-formaldehyde glue, and there are serious health concerns regarding formaldehyde. To minimize the vapors, all particle surfaces and edges should be sealed.

Particleboard can be purchased with coated surfaces or a material can be glued onto it. Surface materials are usually plastic laminates, melamine or wood veneer. Plastic laminates and melamine are smooth surface materials, available in different colors. Laminates include brand-name materials such as Formica and Wilsonart, and they are generally more expensive than melamine. However, even novice woodworkers can glue laminates to particleboard; melamine is fixed to the surface at the factory. Melamine is the most common and affordable surface material; it is a tough plastic-type material that seals the particleboard or MDF and resists wear, chemicals and stains.

Almost any known wood is available as wood veneer. Businesses that specialize in veneers generally stock rare-wood veneers, such as Brazilian Rosewood, or more common woods such as walnut and oak. These veneers are available in sheets and rolls, and they are often sequentially numbered, like pages in a book. This permits matching of grain and color patterns for striking finished appearances. Wood veneer is attached to particleboard or MDF with wood veneer glue, or it's available as factory-attached surfaces.

Other disadvantages of particleboard are that it doesn't hold screws well, it is not moisture resistant and its edges are subject to crumbling if roughly handled. Coated particleboard must be cut with good equipment. Commercial cabinet shops use very large-surface table saws with sliding tables. These saws often have two

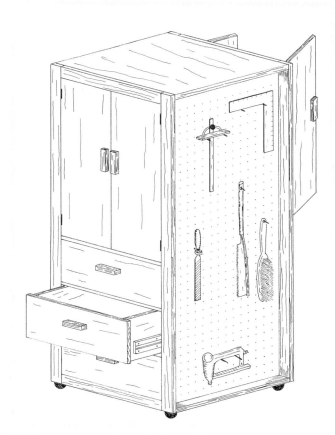

Modular storage station. Includes pegboard side panels, drawers and cabinets.

Side view of modular storage station. Shown are opened doors and adjustable shelf edges. As shown, the station has six drawers.

saw blades, a scoring blade and a sawing blade, which produce a chipfree cut. Smaller, contractor-type table saws might be too small to handle the size and weight of a full sheet of particleboard or MDF. Remember that MDF is heavier than particleboard.

If your table saw is large enough to handle particleboard sheets, you should use a high-quality tungsten-carbide saw blade designed for man-made materials. The generally recommended saw blade has a triple-chip grind; that is, every other tooth has three cutting edges. I use a Forrest Mfg. Co. saw blade

that produces chipfree, clean, sharp edges in melamine-coated particleboard—and it isn't a triple-chip design. This blade has a high alternate top-bevel profile (model Duraline HI A/T). The average alternative top-bevel saw blades have 15° to 25° angles; the Forrest blade has a positive rake with a 40° angle so that as the blade spins down into the bottom melamine surface, it cleanly pierces the material and makes a clean exit cut.

EVALUATING SOLID WOOD Although the list of disadvantages of particleboard may seem overwhelm-

ing, a similar list can be made for solid wood. Durability, toxicity, weight, cutting ability, finishes, cost and availability are all applicable concerns related to solid wood. The relevant point is to know the advantages and disadvantages before working with *any* material.

USING PEGBOARD

If cabinets aren't the type of storage that works best in your workshop, consider covering all wall areas with pegboard. Use tempered hardboard pegboard because it's more durable than the nontempered type: It holds up

Tom Dailey built storage drawers in the heavy-duty frame supporting a metal lathe.

Jon Magill has a mobile base under the table saw. He also installed drawer storage for frequently used table saw and router table accessories.

well under repeated attachment of the metal hangers. Attach ¾″ × 2″ × *necessary length* strips to the wall, attach the pegboard to the strips and then paint the pegboard with a light, nonreflective paint. As you work in a particular area, you will begin to hang tools and accessories relevant to the nearest machine or work area. Pegboard, unlike cabinets and custom storage units, allows for easy workshop rearrangement: Simply remove all tools, accessories and hangers and reposition them in new areas. Additionally, if you move away and remove everything but the pegboard from the workshop, the new owner will have a presentable room covered entirely with an attractive wall covering.

Pegboard Storage Tower

A useful storage option for smaller workshops is a movable storage tower, which looks like a telephone booth on wheels. The sides can be constructed of solid sheeting, pegboard, recessed shelves or drawers. This unit can be rolled to work areas and then stored in a less used area when it's not needed. Because it's a tower, don't store heavy objects in the upper half—keep weighty objects near the base so that it doesn't tip over. Locking wheels are optional, but are worth considering. If the tower is to be left in one place for a prolonged period, it would be safer to lock the wheels.

USING ''WASTED'' SPACE

Many stationary machines, including the table saw, jointer, planer and band saw, sit on dead space; that is, their stands are open-structured tables or sheet-metal boxes that are mostly empty. I suggest that it's a better use of workshop space if the metal-legged stands are replaced with a shop-made storage unit. This undermachine cabinet can accommodate general storage, or it can serve as specialized storage for a particular machine. Any design, simple or complex, can be adapted so that an enclosed table-like cabinet with drawers and doors is both safe and functional. Lockable wheels are optional, although it's often very useful to be able to move a machine for either unusual applications or storage.

Movable Storage Units

A variation of the storage unit on wheels is making a set of movable (no wheels) storage modules, each having the same shape, height, width and depth. They can be set on different-height bases or stacked on each

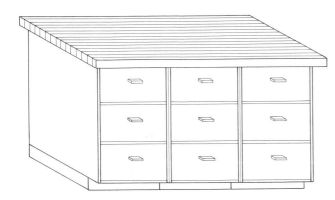

Three modules with a laminated workbench top.

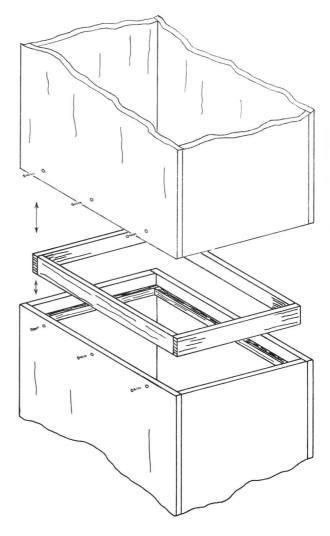

The basic module is shown at far left. This unit is approximately bench height and consists of three drawers. The drawing on the right consists of six basic modules. There are three stacked on each other.

When stacking, secure the modules together using a retainer ring and screws.

other. Build these units to be the same-height as your workbench, table saw or other surfaces so that there is same-height support of oversized materials. The width and depth should be selected to fit your workshop configuration. Using 18″ as an example width, setting a series of 18″-wide storage units side by side produces 3′- and 6′-wide structures. A simple top can be set on the structure, making a very usable work surface. Or another set of units can be set on top of the lower set, producing a wall of storage. I recommend that all storage units be attached to walls once they are positioned. Use long dry-wall screws with fender washers through the storage unit's back and into wall studs. The bonus of this design is that it's possible to reconfigure storage areas as necessary. Adding new units, re-positioning units or taking them with you if you move are all easily accomplished.

LUMBER STORAGE

Lumber storage is the opposite of tool storage. Tools are used and then returned to storage; lumber is in a constant cycle of replenishment, storage and use. Lumber only returns to storage as smaller pieces. Furthermore, lumber sizes and quantities are also in flux, depending on the

Storage of long, thin wood strips and miter-saw work area in the Caswell workshop.

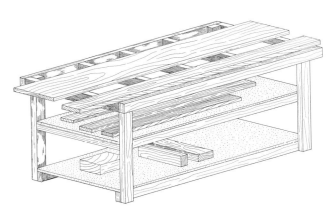

Lumber storage rack. Frame made of 2×4s and particleboard. It can be made in almost any size. Don't make it so tall that it becomes top-heavy and dangerous.

projects at hand. There's particleboard and plywood for cabinet constructions, solid wood for furniture, and random sizes for carvings and lathe turnings. Wood also is brought into the workshop simply because woodworkers enjoy wood. Many times I have stumbled on beautiful pieces of wood that I just couldn't resist, or I've gotten telephone calls concerning the sale of someone's private stock of wood. Inevitably, these various quantities of lumber need storage areas in my workshop. And the constant question is "How much permanent storage should be devoted to lumber that will soon be made into furniture?" Since lumber is transitory, storage should be designed with simplicity, easy access and accommodation of unusual

types and sizes of lumber in mind.

Wall-Hung Rack

For safety and durability, make wall hangers of a suitable thickness. If the total weight of stored lumber is slight (moulding strips, long dowels and thin slats), 2"-thick hangers are adequate. If you plan on storing heavier loads, use 4×4s for the hangers. Use sections of 1"×16" heavy metal pipe for the supports. Drill the support holes through the 4×4 at a slight angle (approximately 4°). Attach the hangers to wall studs with lag bolts and washers. Attach as many hangers as seems reasonable for the load (wall studs are every 16").

Storage Rack

The ideal lumber storage rack should allow access to all four

sides. By being able to walk around a storage rack, you can find and easily remove lumber without having to move an entire stack to get to a board in the back. It's a tiring, time-consuming process to constantly sort through lumber to find the right wood for a project, and boards at the back or bottom of a stack are often overlooked. If you can see the lumber from all sides of the rack, removing it will be simpler. Realistically, most workshops do not have the space for a walk-around rack; lumber is stored against a wall. If space is limited, build a lumber rack with access at its narrower end. That way long boards can be slid in and out with minimum effort.

Make lumber racks according to how much lumber you normally store. It doesn't make

Three wood storage "walls" mounted perpendicular to workshop wall. Secure these wall-to-ceiling joints and anchor them to the floor with steel angle pieces.

sense to build a automobile-size structure if you only store 100 board feet of lumber. However, if you have stacks of lumber to store, build a rack. The framework can be made of 2×4s with ½"-thick particleboard shelves. The rack's size depends on room size and the length of stored lumber. For a small workshop, consider a 4'-wide×10'-long rack. Don't make the rack too tall because it's unsafe to store heavy lumber at elevation, and besides it's difficult to look at lumber that's above shoulder height.

VERTICAL STORAGE RACKS Another version of lumber storage consists of a series of vertical stalls. The framework is attached to the floor, ceiling joists and wall studs. The stalls can be any rea-sonably sized openings so that wood and man-made materials are stored on their ends and are easily accessed.

Storing Sheet Materials

First, a warning regarding sheet materials: plywood, particle-board, MDF, hardboard or any other material that is 4'×8' in size. If your workshop is small, your table saw has a small sur-face area, or you feel that the ma-terial is difficult to handle, don't attempt to cut the full-size sheet on the table saw. Instead, place the sheet on the workbench or sawhorses and cut the sheet to a more manageable size using a circular saw or jigsaw.

If you have a lumber rack, a simple storage solution for sheet materials is to move the rack 6"

to 12" from the wall and then use this "back pocket" for the sheets. Secure a strip of plywood on the floor to facilitate sliding the sheets in and out of the pocket. Sheet materials would then rest against the wall and also be con-tained against the side of the lum-ber rack.

Storing Scrap Wood

Actually, *scrap* isn't the correct word: *Odds and ends* might be a better term. These seemingly useless leftovers are actually a valuable resource. After setting aside the odds and ends, the little that's left is *waste*, the stuff to throw out or burn.

Odds and ends are used for:

- testing machine setup
- determining the look of vari-ous finishing products
- cutting dowel-type plugs to contrast with or complement project wood
- repair work—matching grain and color for antique restoration
- making drawer and door pulls
- making wedges for tenons

A recycled fish crate is used for storing turning blanks.

- small-size scroll saw pieces
- small-size carvings
- small spindle turnings
- toy constructions
- tool handles (files, rasps, lathe tools, carving tools, etc.)
- knife handles
- pieces for workshop jigs and fixtures

Storing odds and ends, cutoff pieces and other irregular-size pieces is perhaps one of the most difficult storage problems in the woodshop. The typical solution, after becoming overwhelmed, is to store the odds and ends haphazardly in bins and boxes. And that means that every time that a small piece of wood is needed, the entire box has to be emptied. Since there is

no rational order regarding the size and shape of smaller pieces, it's difficult to sort and store them by that method. My generalized storage of smaller pieces is by length, color, and, depending upon quantity, sometimes by type of wood. In the end, I have shelves and shallow bins with groupings of "dark" and "light" woods, or groupings of walnut, cherry, oak and maple lengths.

For storing very small pieces (2″ to 8″ in length), I use two wooden boxes that are approximately 2′ × 2′ × 3′ in size. One box is used for storage; the other box is kept empty. When I need a small piece of wood, I sort from the full box into the empty one. If the storage box becomes too full,

I remove the excess and use it for fireplace kindling.

One clever storage system uses various diameter cardboard tubes to store longer pieces. Tubes are generally available in 3″ to 12″ diameters. Cut plywood (or particleboard) disks to fit one tube end and nail in place. The tubes are then placed horizontally on shelves, and pieces slide into them easily. Large-diameter tubes can be found at better hardware stores or at concrete supply houses. These tubes are used as molds for pouring concrete cement foundations. (They are sometimes referred to as *sonotubes*.) Tubes are generally available in 6′ lengths and are easily sawed into 2′ or 3′ sections.

The auxiliary table for this table saw is also used for storing small pieces of wood.

7

POWERING AND LIGHTING THE SHOP EFFECTIVELY

There's no denying the fact that electricity is the fundamental necessity of the modern workshop.

WARNINGS ABOUT ELECTRICITY

Before you begin to do anything with electrical wiring, there are a few cautions. First, never attempt any electrical work if you have doubts about the wiring situation or the consequences of your effort. Second, two agencies you should be aware of are your local building departments (usually city and county) and the utility company. The building department has electrical inspectors who can explain local codes and requirements concerning permits for the work and any necessary inspections. Requirements, regulations and amended versions of the National Electrical

Code (NEC) vary from area to area. It is very important that you follow the codes and guidelines established for your area. The utility company can assist in the location of underground cables and will recommend the correct approach to any electrical service upgrade. Third, you should find a recommended licensed electrical contractor. Often, it's less time-consuming, more economical and safer to have an expert install new wiring, electrical service panels or other custom work. Fourth, electrical work is similar to woodworking: Both require specialized tools and supplies. If you don't have the correct tools, be prepared to rent, buy or borrow them. A visit to an electrical supply store is enough to make you realize that there are scores of supplies, many of

which have to meet your local electrical codes.

EVALUATE YOUR ELECTRICAL NEEDS

There are several starting points in the evaluation of electrical requirements for a workshop. The first, and most obvious, is that if the existing room has a single overhead light with a pull chain and only one or two outlets, the room is probably underpowered for woodworking machinery. Check the electrical service panel for the circuit breaker to the potential workshop location; if there is only one 15- or 20-amp circuit, the service will need upgrading. If you start up a table saw and the lights dim, perhaps you should stop woodworking for a while and upgrade the electrical service.

How you upgrade or install adequate electrical service for a workshop location is somewhat dependent on whether you are remodeling or building a new room. It's certainly more straight-forward installing wiring and out-lets in a new construction. Rout-ing cables through open framework is much simpler than when walls, doors and ceilings are in place.

ELECTRICITY ESSENTIALS

There are many comprehensive books on basic wiring that detail all of the various electrical require-ments and upgrades for a house. Many of these books are written for do-it-yourselfers, so they're easy to read and follow. What I want to address are the specific electrical essentials of the work-shop. These essentials are

- safety
- adequate electrical supply
- 110V and 220V service
- sufficient outlets
- proper lighting

SAFETY RULES

There are two main safety con-siderations: the type required when actually upgrading a sys-tem and the safety of having the correct amperes, cables, outlets, etc., once the upgrading is done. While these may seem similar, they're distinctly different.

The safety of doing upgrading work generally consists of knowl-edge, information, common sense, proper tools and supplies. To safely complete an electrical upgrade requires knowing the electrical requirements of your machinery and tools, the code compliance requirements of out-lets that are in correct locations, use of the proper types and sizes of cables, outlets, etc. If you have any reservations about any of these points, it might be best to call in an electrical contractor. After all, electrical current is invisi-ble—until there is electrical shock or electrical fire.

The first rule: Never work on a *live* circuit. Always disconnect the circuit at the service panel. That means switching the circuit breaker to *off* or removing a screw-in fuse. Remember that the electrical power is still live to the service panel from the power utility lines (either below or above ground). So even if you switch the main power off, the power is still live to the service. It's sort of like closing a dam's spillway: Wa-ter may not be leaving the dam, but there is still water on the other side of the dam.

Be certain that the circuit is off by first turning on a light that's plugged into that circuit. If it goes out when the circuit is switched off, proceed with the next procedure.

It's always a good idea to tell others that you are disconnect-ing a circuit. This is especially im-portant when working at some distance from the service panel. You might even tape a note to the service panel warning others that you are working on the service.

Never work on any electrical fixtures, the service panel, the wiring or anything else electrical when there are wet spots, moist conditions or standing water. Dry the area as much as possible. Open windows and doors to aid in drying damp basements. If there is moisture on the floor, construct a platform of dry boards over the wet areas.

Use the Correct Tools

There are a few common tools that you probably have in the workshop that are useful for elec-trical work.

- mat knife—cutting wallboard and, with the blade barely ex-posed, cutting sheathed cable
- hammer—the obvious; also use to knock out coin-type plugs in switch boxes
- screwdrivers—the obvious
- Allen wrenches—fittings and terminals often are secured with hex screw heads
- Square-drive screwdrivers—many electricians now use screws with square holes in-stead of slot or Phillips heads. Square-drive screws are fast and easy to use.
- tape measure—yes, the obvious

- keyhole saw—for sawing holes in walls and hard-to-reach locations prior to installing boxes or cables
- hacksaw—for sawing conduit to length
- cordless drill with drill bits—the perfect drill when the power is off

A Few Specialized Tools

- engineer's or lineman's pliers—use to twist bare wires together and then cut the last 1/8" off so that the twisted wires fit into a wirenut; large serrated jaws can bend flat metal
- diagonal cutting pliers—for cutting wire; fits in confined locations
- needle nose or snipe-nosed pliers—for picking up and holding small parts in confined locations
- wire strippers—adjustable to different wire gauges for removing insulation
- multipurpose electrician's wire strippers/tool—several features: wire stripper, wire cutter, crimper and bolt cutter
- insulated screwdrivers—entire screwdriver, except blade tip, is coated with insulation
- conduit bender—long-handled device for bending metal conduit to various angles
- fish tape—thin metal line for pulling cable through en-

closed areas; i.e., walls and ceilings
- cable ripper—a cutting device for slitting the sheathing on cable
- voltage tester—for testing circuits and wires to determine whether they're live, or hot
- continuity tester—for determining whether a circuit is open or has a short circuit; used when the power is off
- ground tester (or GFI, ground fault interrupter tester)—a plug-like device that inserts into an outlet and indicates whether correct ground exists
- electronic metal and voltage detector—a device similar to stud finder that locates any metal objects and detects AC voltage within wall

Note: It's a good idea to have insulated handles on pliers and other metal tools. However, don't rely on insulated tools as the only safety precaution: Always turn circuits off before working on them.

ELECTRICAL SUPPLIES

There are many common electrical items to choose for upgrades. However, be certain that they are approved or meet local building codes. If you aren't sure of these items, it's best to consult certified experts. There are too many choices—guessing which part or wire size to use is the wrong approach.

Wire principally is a single strand of conductive metal enclosed with insulation. *Cord* is stranded wires protected by insulation. It can consist of two or three stranded wires within the insulation and is used for appliances, lamps, etc. *Cable* has two or more color-coded insulated wires that are protected by sheathing. In the United States the colors of the individual wires are agreed upon: Black or red is the power, or hot, wire; white or gray is the neutral wire; and green or green with a yellow stripe is the ground wire. Sometimes the ground wire is a single uninsulated copper wire.

Wire Size and Type

It's very important to use the correct wire size and type when upgrading an electrical system. Local codes will specify what sorts of cable and cable conduits are permitted in your area.

WIRE TYPES *Type NM* has a thermoplastic insulation and is capable of withstanding a wide range of temperatures. It's used for most household circuits.

Type UF (underground feed cable) is waterproof and is used for damp and outdoor locations.

Type USE (underground service entrance) is used for underground or overhead service entrance and direct burial to garages and workshops.

Type THW is used for outdoor hanging or indoor conduit as service entrance cables and for conduit to a subpanel.

Nonmetallic (NM) cable is the most common plastic-sheathed cable. It's often referred to as Romex, which is a trade name. The sheath is usually moisture resistant and flame retardant. Normally, there are insulated power wires and a bare ground wire inside of the sheath.

Armored cable, also referred to by the trade name BX cable, has an outer armored layer, usually flexible galvanized steel, that often contains two or three wires wrapped in paper.

Conduit is usually galvanized steel or plastic pipe. It's generally available in ½", ¾", 1" and 1¼" diameters. The correct size to use depends on the diameter and number of wires inside the conduit.

WIRE SIZE Wire size, basically the diameter of the wire excluding insulation, is extremely important when upgrading an electrical system. First, there are standard reference numbers, usually printed on the outside of wire insulation, that are based on the American Wire Gauge (AWG) system. Gauge numbers are inverse to their size; that is, the smaller the number, the larger the wire diameter. The maximum current that a wire can safely manage is

stated in amperes (amps). Wire diameter and the amount of amperes are directly related. Smaller diameter wires have greater resistance to electrical current flow; consequently, as the current flow increases, so do friction and heat. Avoid melting wires and electrical fires by using larger diameter wires for heavier electrical needs.

Common copper house wire (by gauge) and its ampere ratings:

No. 18	7 amperes
No. 16	10 amperes
No. 14	15 amperes
No. 12	20 amperes
No. 10	30 amperes
No. 8	40 amperes
No. 6	55 amperes

CALCULATING ELECTRICAL USAGE IN THE WORKSHOP

Remember, no matter what electrical circuits or subpanels are added to the house's electrical service, the total house load must not exceed the service rating. Generally, older homes having no electrical modernization have 100-amp services. Newer homes generally have 200-amp services. If you are not certain about the service, look at the main circuit breaker in the service panel—it should be labeled. If you have 100-amp service, I would suggest consulting with both the utility company and a licensed electrician regarding upgrading to a 200-amp service.

The woodshop is probably going to have machines and power tools, unless, of course, you're taken with the joy of only working with hand tools. Generally, workshops will have one woodworker using no more than two machines at one time (table saw and dust collector; drill press and vacuum). The advantage of this is that the electrical system isn't going to need to support the simultaneous operation of all the workshop's machinery. As you plan the electrical layout, make a best guess as to the frequency of use of tools and machines. Not only will this aid in determining circuit requirements, but it will also aid in planning the placement

NUMBER OF WIRES WITHIN A CONDUIT*

Wire Size	½" conduit	¾" conduit	1" conduit	1¼" conduit
14	4	6	9	9
12	3	5	8	9
10	1	4	7	9
8	1	3	4	7
6	1	1	3	4

*Actual number is also governed by local codes

A subpanel installed near the main circuit breaker panel.

of circuit breakers and wire. The exception to this is the dust collector, which is also 220V. However, because it's operated simultaneously with each of the stationary machines, there was no choice—it required its own circuit.

The National Electrical Code sets minimum capacities regarding use and amperage for circuits.

- Small appliances—20 amperes
- General lighting—15 or 20 amperes
- Stationary tools—multiply the machine's amperage by 125%.

The 125% factors the electrical surge that occurs when a machine is first switched on. For example, a 12″ planer rated at 15 amps ($1.25 \times 15 = 18.75$) will require a 20-amp circuit.

OUTLETS, SWITCHES AND PLUGS

Until the day comes that we can use tools powered by wireless telemetry, workshops will need outlets and switches. When designing a new electrical layout, placement of outlets and switches requires planning, guesswork and a bit of luck. The reality of workshops is that work projects, new machines, relocation of cabinets, stacks of lumber and other fluctuating events will block existing outlets and switches from access. Often,

of outlets. The reality of upgrading workshop electrical systems is that it's often easier to install separate outlets on separate circuits than to have one circuit with multiple outlets. For example, in my workshop I have three machines requiring 220V service: the table saw, jointer/planer and band saw. Rarely, if ever, are two machines running at the same time. So it's

possible for the three machines to have their outlets wired to the same circuit. However, these machines are located in different areas of the workshop, and it was much easier to install outlets at each of the machine locations and route wires through one or more conduits. Since there was adequate space in the subpanel, it was a straightforward addition

TYPICAL MACHINE AND TOOL AMPERAGE RATINGS
(machines and tools are 110-120V, with exceptions noted)

Machine	Tool Amperage
10" Table saw	8.3@230V
10" Contractor's table saw	12.8
14" Band saw (½ hp)	9
10" Radial arm saw	11/5.5@120/240V
12" Miter saw	13
6" Jointer	9.5
12" Planer	15
Drill press	6
6"×48" Sander	8.4@240V
12" Lathe (¾ hp)	11.4
Scroll saw	1.3
Dust collector (2 bag)	16/8@115/230V
Dust collector (4 bag)	17@230V
20 gal. Shop vacuum	10.5
3½ hp Air compressor	15
Router, (1 hp)	6.8
Router, (3 hp)	15
4"×24" Belt sander	10.5
Plate jointer	6.5
Finish sander	1.7
Spindle sander	3.5
Shaper (2 hp)	16/8@110/220V
⅜" Hand drill	4
Bench grinder	6
1"×30" Strip sander	2.6
Jigsaw	4.8
Circular saw	13
Heat gun	14
Bench-top mortiser	6
HVLP spray gun turbine	11.5

well-thought-out locations aren't that handy once the workshop is used. The ideal situation is never having to use extension cords because you have outlets wherever you work. This can be accomplished simply by locating outlets three to five feet apart throughout the workshop, including the ceiling. This may seem excessive, but it's not. There are too many work conditions that occur away from the workbench area: using a vacuum, sander, plate joiner, rotary carving tool or heat gun are but a few of the applications possible.

There are two scenarios for installing outlets. If the workshop area is a new construction, wires should be installed within the wall framework. If wall coverings are already in place, outlets can be installed on the outside of the wall surface if metal conduit and metal outlet boxes are used. Always check your local electrical codes concerning this type of installation. External conduit adds flexibility to designing and locating outlets, simply because conduit can be routed just about anywhere. Metal conduit pipe is easily bent to a variety of shapes and angles with a conduit bender. One option for the 90° bend at corners is to use short pre-bent right-angle conduit pieces. These are attached to the straight conduit with sleeve connectors. Conduit pipe can be cut wherever necessary and outlets installed.

Steven Gray has an unusual (for the home workshop, that is) electrical system. His workshop features overhead electrical rails. These "feed" rails are connected to the main power panel. What is unique is that "trolleys" slide within the rails, and lights or AC switches can be attached to the trolleys. The feed rail is both 110V and 220V. And both voltages are usable, depending on how the contact trolley wheels are aligned within the feed rail. It's a very neat system, with movable electrical items all in one track, both 110V and 220V outlets and different types of lighting.

Acceptable Outlets
- Grounded 3-prong, 120V, 15 amp
- Grounded 3-prong, 120V, 20 amp
- Ground fault circuit

Overhead electric feed rail in Steven Gray's workshop.

Close-up view of the electric feed rail.

Switches and plugs are installed on the electrical feed rail system.

Various lights are installed on an electrical feed rail system.

interrupter, 120V, 15 and 20 amp
- Grounded 3-prong, 220/240V

Note: Ungrounded 2-prong, 120V receptacles are unacceptable for shop use.

Use grounded 3-prong, 20-amp outlets in the workshop. This will accommodate most woodworking tools (see tool amperage chart). If an existing workshop has ungrounded 2-prong outlets, turn off the main power and replace the old outlets with grounded outlets. If there isn't a ground wire to the outlet, attach one from the outlet to the receptacle box or the nearest cold water pipe. Check

that the ground is functional by using a ground tester.

Ground fault circuit interrupter outlets (GFI) are designed to protect you from shock. GFI outlets monitor current; if the incoming and outgoing currents aren't the same, the GFI instantly cuts off the electricity (in $\frac{1}{40}$ second). GFI will trip if there is a ground fault of 0.005 amps. GFI outlets are found in newer houses, generally in bathrooms and outdoor locations where someone may have wet hands and feet. If you are installing outlets in damp basements or

around sinks, you should install GFI units. As with all electrical installations, check local codes or hire a licensed electrician if you have any questions regarding the installation.

Switches

Switches are rated according to amperage and voltage, so it's important to choose the correct switch for compatibility with circuits, wire and outlets.

There are four basic types of switches:
- Single-pole switches have two terminals, one for the incoming hot wire and one for the outgoing hot wire. The switch toggle is imprinted with *ON/OFF*.
- Double-pole switches have four terminals and are used primarily for 240V circuits. The switch toggle is imprinted with *ON/OFF*.
- Three-way switches have

three terminals. One terminal is labeled *COM* (common), and the hot wire is connected to this terminal; the other two terminals are switch leads. Two three-way switches are used to control a circuit from two different locations. The toggle has no *ON/OFF* imprint.

■ Four-way switches have four terminals and are used with two three-way switches to control a circuit from more than two locations. The toggle has no *ON/OFF* imprint.

Plugs

Woodworkers, please raise your hand if you *always* go to the outlet and carefully grip the plug to unplug it. Now raise your hand if you occasionally unplug a tool by pulling the cord. The point is, plugs receive quite a lot of use and wear. When plugs need replacing, replace them with dead-front plugs. This type of plug has no exposed wires or screws, and the prongs are surrounded by smooth plastic. If there are screws on the plate surrounding the prongs, they are recessed and are only for securing the plug body together.

If you are attaching wires to a 125V plug with three prongs, connect the black wire to the brass terminal, the white wire to the silver terminal and the green wire to the green or gray terminal.

Polarized plugs are identified by having one brass prong (hot) and one silver prong with a wider tip. The plug is designed to fit into an outlet in only one direction. This plug is commonly installed on smaller appliances and woodworking tools.

LIGHTING THE WOODSHOP

There seem to be two distinct types of lighting in most workshops: fluorescent lighting and a minimal use of all other types of lighting. I'm drawn to conclude that fluorescent lighting is the most used simply because it's inexpensive, commonly available at most hardware stores and thought to be the best for woodworking applications. Other lighting is thought to be most useful only in standard home applications and not in the woodshop.

Workshop lighting is a woefully neglected aspect of today's woodworking. There is a cornucopia of aftermarket improvements to almost everything electric within the workshop except lighting. Lighting stores and hardware stores usually have jumbled lighting displays, making it nearly impossible to view and judge lighting fixtures one at a time. The one exception I've found is a GE display of different fluorescent lamps. This display is a set of identical photographs, individually set in a series of re-

cessed boxes, each lit by a different fluorescent lamp. This display nicely reveals the color-rendering differences of fluorescent lamps.

Unfortunately, few light fixtures seem to be designed specifically for woodshops. Those that are tend to be either sterile-looking white metal devices or cheap-looking clip-on reflector hoods. This simply means that it's up to the woodworker to solve workshop lighting questions through both personal experience and research. Trial and error may seem like a difficult path to follow, but it does allow you to customize your workshop.

When evaluating lights and fixtures, consider that there are several key elements to using light: color, shadow, contrast and reflection. These are the products of lighting that we see in both dynamic and subtle ways. They give usefulness, meaning and emotional cohesiveness to woodworking. Many artists refer to the process of their work as "painting with light." Woodworkers should also control and use light for both room lighting and artistic, aesthetic reasons.

Color is perhaps the most subjective and difficult aspect of light. A simple request proves this point: Define "red." We may generally agree on the notion that tomatoes, apples and rubies are red, but it's extremely difficult to describe a particular color and have general agreement on it: Color perception is in the eye of the beholder. Furthermore, location, situation and light source will change a color. For example, if a person is holding an apple and standing in the glow of sunset, the apple will look different (warmer) than when it's sitting on a workbench situated under fluorescent lights (cooler). And if the apple is placed under a green light, it will change color once again—it will appear grayish. Imagine the effect that lighting will have if a workpiece of dark cherry is subjected to warm or cool lights. Will that "golden oak" stain look yellowish or greenish?

Elements That Offer Control Over Color

The problem isn't just that color perception is subjective; it's often that a woodworker and client can't see the same color. Suppose that you restore a Stickley chair using only fluorescent lights, and the client places the chair so that it's lit by an incandescent lamp. Color for a Stickley piece is very important. In fact, collectors pay such close attention to the color that the value of the piece and its color are connected. The chair will appear differently under those various lights—and the client probably won't be happy. This difference of color is a function of wave-

length variations. Different lighting will have warmer or cooler colors, with many different combinations of spectral differences.

Warmer light is often thought of as the daylight at sunset or the light from an incandescent bulb. Cooler light is the light of the moon, an overcast sky or fluorescent light.

One commonly used method of describing the differences in light is the reference to temperature, expressed in degrees Kelvin (K). This scale is invaluable for selecting light to match your needs. Generally, lower degrees Kelvin represents a warmer appearance, and higher degrees Kelvin represents a cooler look.

Note: The Kelvin reference, while very useful, is somewhat of a "ballpark" number. The visual color of an object will be influenced by such things as the age and darkening of a bulb or by the fact that two different lights (natural and warm) may have the same Kelvin value but different color renderings.

If your work demands color-balanced conditions so that the workpiece color is "true," the workshop lighting system must be designed accordingly. The most obvious solution is to have windows and skylights so that natural light floods the work area. If that's impossible (in basements, garages and interior rooms), a mixture of different fluo-

rescent and incandescent lights might be the solution.

Shadow, Reflection and Contrast

One of the most vexing lighting assignments I had in art school was to place an egg on a white surface that also had a white background and, using a single photoflood lamp, light the egg so that there was complete definition of the egg and no "bleeding" of white from the egg to the surface or background. After more than a few hours, I thought that I had a workable scene. The problem was one of degree, too much or too little shadow, too much or not enough reflection and too much or too little contrast. Lighting focused straight on from the camera produced flat light; lighting from the side produced strong shadows; and diffuse lighting softened the image but at times did not produce any tonal separation. And all of these lighting setups were further changed if the light was close to or far from the subject.

In the workshop, the location, type and intensity of lights will produce a continuum of unacceptable and acceptable lighting conditions. Work area illumination requires careful light placement so that the area is shadow free. Obviously it's possible to cover every square inch of ceiling with lights, but that's *very* inefficient. A better method

DEGREES KELVIN RATINGS

Daylight at sunrise	1800 K
Incandescent lamp (tungsten)	2600 K
Halogen lamp	3200 K
Warm white fluorescent lamp	3000 K
Cool white fluorescent lamp	4200 K
Daylight at noon	5000 K
*Photoflood lamp (tungsten)	3200 to 3400 K
*Photoflood lamp (daylight)	4800 to 5400 K
*Photo strobe (electric flash)	5200 to 5400 K
*Daylight-balanced film	5000 to 5400 K
"Sunshine" fluorescent lamp	5000 K
"Daylight" fluorescent lamp	6500 K

*Degrees Kelvin is also useful if you are photographing your woodworking. The type of lights or strobes and film used will warm or cool the subject.

is using the correct lights at their correct location. Flat lighting can be beneficial to a cabinetmaker wanting to see dovetail layout lines clearly. However, flat lighting isn't very useful for woodcarving. Lighting that is 45° to 90° to the carving will create better and more useful shadows that enhance the carving process. The texture and incisions from carving tools are very visible, and the carver can use the shadows to enliven details. If a carver knows the location and lighting conditions of the site where a large carving will finally reside, lights can be temporarily placed in the workshop to duplicate that lighting. This preparation can spare the carver future problems. For example, a large statue of a Greek warrior will be permanently lit by two overhead spotlights. Knowing this, the carver can dramatize specific features,

such as the helmet against the skin or the shape of a flowing cape. The carver can also shape facial features, such as the nose and eyebrows, so that the face isn't ruined by ugly shadows.

Generally, it's best to locate light fixtures so that light falls directly over a work area. If there are numerous fluorescent lights throughout a work area, the diffuse light should limit shadowing. If, for example, there's a fluorescent light positioned above and behind someone at a workbench (or table saw), there will be shadows in the work area. This will occur even with the diffuse lighting of numerous fluorescent lights. To avoid this problem at the workbench, I have placed one double 8' fluorescent light fixture above the workbench, and I have three double 8' fluorescent light fixtures positioned perpendicular to the workbench

and slightly behind and above the work side of the bench. These fixtures are approximately 5' apart and the ceiling height is 9'. The result is that I have diffuse, shadow-free lighting at the workbench.

Ceiling height, or the distance from the light to the work area, is important. The general rule is that for any type of light (direct or diffuse, incandescent or fluorescent), the closer to the work area, the stronger the shadows. The opposite is also true: The more distance between the light and the work area, the weaker the shadows.

Types of Lamps

There are three main types of lamps/lights for use in the workshop: tungsten-filament lamps, halogen lamps and fluorescent lighting.

TUNGSTEN-FILAMENT BULBS Tungsten-filament bulbs are the most common bulbs found in homes. These are made of clear, frosted or tinted glass. Tungsten lamps are the most common lamps because their light is similar to the warm tone of natural light and because they have history on their side—this is the bulb that Edison invented. Tungsten bulbs are everywhere, and it's easy to change lighting conditions by simply replacing one bulb with another type of tungsten bulb. Clear bulbs produce a bright and more contrasting type of lighting. Frosted bulbs produce a diffused lighting; tinted bulbs can add a diffuse warmth to the environment. Spotlights and floodlights are also tungsten bulbs. These have body shapes and front lenses that either focus or diffuse the light. Generally, the beam angle is 15° to 25° for spotlights and 30° to 75° for floodlights.

HALOGEN LAMPS What we refer to as halogen lamps are actually tungsten-halogen lamps. There are two basic halogen lamp types: low voltage and standard line voltage. Low-voltage halogen lamps require a transformer and operate at both lower voltage and lower wattage than standard-line-voltage halogen lamps. They are usually designed as reflectors, allowing them to be directed at specific work areas. Low-voltage halogen lamps are relatively small and lend themselves to use in recessed fixtures. Generally, the beam angle from the reflector is 5° to 30°.

Standard-line-voltage halogen lamps are more efficient than standard incandescent tungsten lamps, but they have the disadvantages of expense and high temperatures. Light fixtures must be capable of dissipating heat, and line-voltage halogen lamps should be kept away from any

flammable materials—not a simple task in the woodshop. Recently there have been safety notices regarding fires being caused by certain styles of line-voltage halogen lamps, and screens have been made available for retrofitting on the lamp housing to keep cloth, paper and other flammable materials from touching the bulb. Furthermore, avoid touching the bulb with your bare hands because skin oil will affect the bulb and shorten its lifespan.

FLUORESCENT LAMPS There is a distinct division between home and commercial lighting: Most homes have tungsten lighting, and most businesses use fluorescent lighting. The reasons for this difference are both historical and economical. Simplistically, houses have always been built and designed with incandescent lights as the principal lighting. What we can learn from commercial use is that fluorescent lighting is a source of low-cost, efficient diffused lighting. As a dramatic comparison, tungsten bulbs have an average life of 750 to 1250 hours; fluorescent lights have an average life of 20,000 hours.

Fluorescent lamps are available in a variety of lengths, shapes and colors to satisfy any workshop requirement. There are different color sensitivities,

ranging from cool to warm white. Before purchasing the different varieties of fluorescent lights, make sure that the lamp and the fixture are compatible by checking the lamp's wattage with that of the ballast.

Poor-quality fluorescent lights have created a bad reputation for better quality fluorescent lights. Typical problems associated with low-quality fluorescent lights are leaking ballasts, humming or vibration noise and pulsing light. These are generally not problems in better made units.

One problem that occurs in workshops is that of long boards reaching fluorescent lights. Lights above workbenches and table saws are often hit, showering the woodworker with glass particles. To avoid this, clear plastic sleeves or tubes are available to fit fluorescent lamps. If the lamp is hit and breaks, the glass shards remain in the plastic sleeve.

TYPES OF FLUORESCENT LAMPS When shopping for fluorescent lamps, find a hardware or electrical supply store that stocks a full array of lamp types. There are at least eight different types of fluorescent lights. Store displays and product packaging should furnish lamp designations, including references to color rendering, degrees Kelvin, watts and lumens. Product names such as

TYPICAL FLOURESCENT LIGHTS

	Kelvin	Lumens*	Watts	CRI**
Sunshine	5000 K.	2250	40	90
Daylight Delux	6500 K.	2250	40	84
SP-35, moderate white	3500 K.	3200	40	73
Kitchen & Bath	3000 K.	3200	40	70
Residential/Shoplight	4100 K.	3150	40	72
SP-41, cool white	4150 K.	3200	40	42

* Lumens is a unit of measurement that expresses the total quantity of light given off by a light source. For practical purposes, if comparing incandescent and fluorescent light, fluorescent lights use much less energy than incandescent bulbs and still produce similar or better light levels.

- 75 watt incandescent bulb is 1190 lumens
- 100 watt incandescent bulb is 1710 lumens
- 20 watt fluorescent light is 1200 lumens
- 32 watt fluorescent light is 3050 lumens

** *Color rendering index* (CRI) is a measurment of color shift when an object is illuminated by a light. CRI ranges from 1 to 100, with natural daylight and incandescent light equal to 100. Therefore, lights with a higher CRI produce more natural colors.

"cool white" or "warm white" are older designations. To comply with newer U.S. government standards regarding fluorescent lights, companies have had to redesign lights. Since the newer versions of "cool white" are different from the older product, newer product names were necessary. Hence, "Sunshine" or "SP-41."

High-Intensity-Discharge Lamps

This lamp wasn't mentioned earlier because it is a fairly new type of lamp and is not yet commonly used. High-intensity-discharge lamps (HID) types are metal halide lamps, mercury lamps and high-pressure sodium lamps. These have primarily been used for industrial purposes, but are slowly being accepted for other uses (mostly for architectural and security purposes). There are disadvantages to using HID lamps: They require warming up and cooling down periods when they are turned on and off, and they produce a bluish light that gives an unfamiliar coloring to most things, including woodworking projects. Currently, the metal halide lamps are the only HID lamps that approach normal colorization. The conclusion about HID lamps is that even though they are energy efficient, until there's better color rendering and fixture configuration, they aren't useful for the workshop.

8

IMPLEMENTING YOUR DUST COLLECTION SYSTEM

It's noteworthy that the original Shaker sect designed their now-famous furniture because of the desire for clean rooms.

SHOP WASTE

If you are using machines and sanding products for woodworking, you are making at least two kinds of waste products: debris that settles on surfaces and airborne particles. Both are difficult to pick up or wipe away, and both require some sort of air movement to remove them.

If you work exclusively with hand tools—hand saws, hand planes, chisels and scrapers—the principal waste will be solid chunks and sawdust mostly deposited on the floor, thus making brooms and dustpans the ideal cleanup tools.

MANAGING SHOP WASTE

If you use machines and sandpaper, however, there are several basic solutions to workshop waste management:

1. Remove floor debris with a broom or shop vacuum.
2. Catch machine-made dust and chips at the source with a dust collector.
3. Filter airborne particles with an air filtration system—or wear a filter mask.
4. Work in a wind tunnel so that all debris and light objects are blown out a door and into a neighbor's yard.

The only other option is to work in piles and clouds of chips and dust.

I have seen few totally dust- and chip-free woodshops. Most woodworkers make some sort of effort to remove most of the debris. Almost all workshops now have some sort of dust collection system, but very few have air filtration systems. Additionally, even with operational dust collectors, there is dust in most workshops. Surprisingly, few woodworkers use filter masks, and I've found several workshops that rely on air flow from open doors and windows to minimize air-suspended particle dust.

There are many sizes and types of dust collectors and air filtration systems in the marketplace. There are readily available dust collectors powerful enough to have three separate 25'-long ducts and to simultaneously remove debris from three separate machines. Additionally, there are many magazine articles detailing how to build everything from collector duct systems to air filtration systems. Over the past ten years there has been considerable interest in the process of duct collection and air filtration.

Why Are Workshops Still Dusty?

The reasons why there are so many dusty workshops is rather complicated.

- There are those who still don't care about the hazardous or unsafe nature of dust. It's a strange mind-set, based on a perception that since woodworking tools and machines make chips and dust, the woodworker should just let the stuff fall where it may. This perception also falsely equates productivity with the amount of dust and chips on the floor (and everywhere else): The myth that a busy workshop is a dusty workshop still exists.

- Another misguided notion about dust collection is that home workshops don't have the same volumes of productivity as professional workshops, hence there is less dust. The Occupational Safety and Health Administration (OSHA) has rules and standards for dust levels in commercial workshops and standards about air quality, safety equipment, proper installation of dust collectors and many other issues relat-

ing to the hazardous nature of dust. The wrong-thinking opposing argument is that since the home workshop is not regulated by OSHA, proper dust management equipment isn't necessary.

- Collectors and filtration systems aren't thought of as primary machines, such as a table saw or a router. Dust collectors don't help to cut better edges or make better dovetails. It's easy to think of dust collectors as part of the group of objects that we all own but aren't overly enthusiastic about: lawn rakes, house vacuums, floor mops and window squeegees. Most woodworkers don't wake up in the morning saying, "I can't wait to go to the workshop and turn on the dust collector!"

- Dust collection systems aren't cheap. A basic dust collector costs from $300 to $1000. Four-inch-diameter ductwork costs approximately $2 to $4 per foot. Fittings, such as elbows, reducers, shutoff gates and Y and T fittings cost $10 to $20 each, and replacement filter bags cost $25 to $75.

- Cost is often the only factor considered when purchasing a dust collector. There are numerous low-priced collectors that are popular simply

because they are inexpensive. To be fair, some of these units probably are adequate if they only have 6' of hose and are hooked to a single machine. In order for manufacturers to make low-cost collectors, they often simplify the collector's frame size, use low-quality impellers, include small-capacity filter bags (and also use low-quality filter material) and install inexpensive (and lower hp) motors.

- Dust collection and air filtration systems are frequently either installed incorrectly or are inadequate for the volume of debris produced. Very often the technical specifications of dust collectors aren't well understood, and it's critical to understand certain technical information when purchasing a dust collector.

DUST COLLECTION BASICS

There are few noteworthy technical considerations specific to dust collection.

- SP (static pressure) is resistance to air in a duct and is measured in inches of water. *Resistance* is often referred to as *friction*.

- CFM (cubic feet per minute) is air volume.

- FPM (feet per minute) is air velocity.

The principal question is: How do you know if a dust collector is installed correctly and whether it can efficiently remove debris? Several important variables affect the performance of any collector.

- technical specifications (hp and CFM)
- distance from the collector to a given machine (duct run)
- number of fittings
- smoothness within the duct system
- diameter of duct
- number of machines

Dust System Considerations

Dust collectors and air filtration systems need to be integrated into the entire workshop. In fact, a case could be made that the dust collection system should be one of the first installations within a workshop, and all machines and other features should be installed subsequently. Consider that when a new house is being constructed and the framing is finished, plumbing and electrical components are installed. Ideally, that is how dust collectors should be viewed. However, most woodworkers usually purchase a dust collector after they start generating mounds of debris from their machines. Then the dust collector is retrofitted to the workshop.

Very few machines are adequately designed for dust con-

trol. To make a dust collection system functional, it must be fitted to machines so that all dust and chips are collected. This is a fundamental weakness of most workshop collection systems. Few factory machine hookups are efficient. It seems that manufacturers, in general, view dust collection as an afterthought. Consider the power tools that produce dispersed dust: planers, routers, all sanders, scroll saws, plate jointers and table saws. How many of these machines are designed with high-quality connections for dust collecting? For example, an efficient table saw dust collection system should have two collection areas: The area below the table

Drill press table in Bill Stankus's workshop featuring different table inserts for different diameter sanding drums. Fence has holder for vacuum hose.

Sanding drum lowered into table and vacuum hose mounted on top of table.

should have a collection enclosure close to the saw blade, and there should also be collection above the saw blade, preferably integrated with the blade guard. Unfortunately, these features mostly exist on the more expensive table saws.

Most experienced woodworkers eventually construct collection hookups for their machines. Well-established workshops often have all sorts of shop-made fittings and specialized hookups on machines.

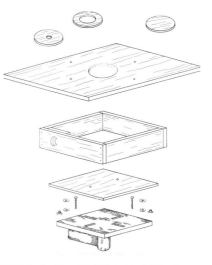

Exploded view of drill press table; frame has hole for vacuum hose. Top surface has center hole with rabbeted edge for holding discs. Discs have different-size cutouts to accommodate sanding drums.

Sanding drum lowered into table and vacuum hose mounted to lower box.

These are usually made of plywood or particleboard, and sometimes acrylic-type plastics, and they are characterized by form-fitting the machine's cutting area, dust chute or wood ejection area.

LOCATING THE DUST COLLECTING AND AIR FILTRATION SYSTEMS

As an analogy, most woodworkers locate dust collectors much like the antiquated houses that were built before indoor plumbing and electricity. When these "new" conveniences were first installed in houses, they were attached to the outside of walls. (Antique tool collectors now prize the hand planes used to make channels in moulding for the exterior attachment of electri-

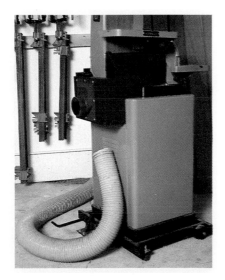

In order to collect dust at the sanding machine, I built a housing (plywood) that encompassed both disc and belt sanding ports. Housing also encloses belt beneath the table. Plastic fitting for the dust hose is available at most hardware stores.

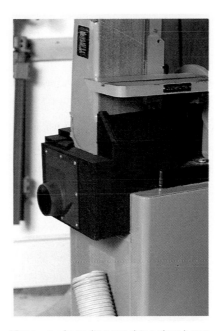

Close-up of sanding machine dust hose housing.

John MacKenzie has under-floor dust collection ductwork.

cal wires.) A modern person would never consider having electrical wires exposed and running around the outside of doors and moulding, nor having water pipes visible in a kitchen or bath. Yet that same modern person will generally not think that retrofitted and exposed dust collection ductwork is inappropriate. I realize that there are many reasons for exposed duct systems:

- basement workshops with concrete walls
- using portable collectors with a short hose
- ease in suspending ductwork from rafters (joists, etc.)
- exposed ductwork is less expensive to install

However, new workshops are being constructed that integrate duct systems into walls and un-

der flooring. This approach requires the same mind-set that's used to install water pipes and electrical wiring. That is, there must be precise design-planning of the system. Like an electrical circuit box or water heater, the dust collector must have a fixed location. This location should be somewhat removed from the general work area of the workshop, and it should be accessible for cleaning. Furthermore, the number and location of machines should be determined prior to building the system.

I suppose it's reasonable to ask, "What's the gain of having a ductwork system built into walls and flooring?" The principal answer is that an internal ductwork system is out of the way, and consequently wall and floor space is freed up and made available for other uses. Most workshops are small, and every visible surface is used for some sort of storage. Long expanses of 4"-diameter, horizontally mounted cylinders complicate the placement of cabinets, lumber storage, lighting and everything else required in the woodshop. Second, machines that are located in the central workshop area and away from any wall create a complication regarding ducts. For example, a table saw in such a location that is hooked up to an exposed duct system will have a duct or hose resting on the floor. This will make maneuvering large or heavy objects difficult. Walking over exposed ductwork is one step away from tripping. Furthermore, the ductwork itself will eventually be damaged by being stepped on or by heavy objects falling on it. In fact, having a duct or hose located below floor level for a table saw is enough of a justification for such a system. That's because, of all the principal workshop machinery, the table saw probably has the most awkward duct or hose arrangement. This is due to the fact that table saws have dust fittings at floor level, and the saws are generally situated in open areas, away from walls. When machines are located near walls, machines then have a back (unused) side, making is easier to

have ductwork that is out of the way installed. It's also difficult to have ducts and hose connections that drop from ceiling areas to the centrally located table saw. These perpendicular hoses will be in the way of lumber, and they create safety problems when cutting materials. (The material being cut can bump into the ductwork and be thrust back toward the blade and the operator.)

Requirements for an Internal Dust Collection System

- Existing workshops may be impossible to retrofit with an internal dust system unless there is extensive remodeling. Ducts are usually from 4" to 10" in diameter, and this means that systems destined for walls, ceilings and floors require sufficient open areas to accommodate these dimensions.

- If walls are not to be remodeled, wood enclosures can be made so that ducts are enclosed. This wood box can be located either at the wall/ceiling interface or the wall/floor interface. At either location, the ductwork is enclosed and safe from bumps and damage. Furthermore, these wood enclosures can be easily integrated with cabinets and other storage units.

- Ductwork systems that include drop-downs from the

ceiling area are somewhat easier to install, if there is sufficient room above joists or there is attic space. Install metal ductwork systems similar to central heating and air conditioning ducts. However, duct drop-downs in the middle of a room should always be considered a nuisance; that is, drop downs probably will be in the way of other workshop functions (moving lumber, etc.).

- In the floor, ductwork has the most to offer in both usefulness and in the degree of difficulty in installation. If there is sufficient floor-to-ceiling height in the workshop, the most straightforward solution is to construct a subfloor; that is, build a new floor above the existing floor so that there is space for the duct system. The new subfloor should be stoutly constructed to support the heavy loads of machines and lumber. However, the real bonus is that ducts can be brought up through the floor next to a machine, or even within a machine's cavity. This will minimize tripping over and/or bumping ducts and hoses.

If a new workshop is being constructed and concrete floors are to be poured, there are several considerations for ductwork below the floor. The basic room design must include adequate floor thickness and floor-to-ceiling height. Duct channels must be created with forms and poured cement. Instead of a single continuous floor surface, it will be necessary to carefully pour cement in different areas between forms and to ensure those areas are flat and true to each other. Once the concrete is hard, ductwork is placed in these channels and the open channel is covered with wood, brick or concrete blocks.

The very nature of workshop design is constant change and the incorporation of new ideas, products and evolution. And although the marketplace is now filled with a variety of similar dust collectors, the use and setup of those dust collectors is changing. It wasn't that long ago that few workshops had any dust collection whatsoever. Now we are using dust collection systems and are attempting to customize them to our individual workshops. Presently, it may be adequate to use dust collectors in the familiar way: using metal ductwork attached to walls and ceilings, with a short length of flexible hose attached to a machine. In the near future, more and more workshops will be set up with more efficient duct systems hidden in walls, the ceiling and the floors. Just as there was no interest in air filtration systems 20 years ago, the integrated duct system will undoubtly be part of future workshops.

SETTING UP DUST COLLECTION AND AIR FILTRATION SYSTEMS

Gather Information

Use magazine advertisements as the first source of information and request technical information from the manufacturers and retailers that supply the collection and filtration systems. Request information about dust collectors, filtration systems, ductwork, flexible hoses, remote on/off devices, high-efficiency filter bags and grounding kits.

Once you have gathered your information, make comparison charts and include:

- Model
- Motor hp
- Motor repair service is in what country?
- Amperes
- Voltage
- CFM (maximum)
- Static pressure
- dBA at 5 ft. (dBA is a unit of measurement that expresses the relative intensity of sound. The least perceptible sound to pain level sound ranges from 0 to about 130 dBA.)
- Hose diameter hookup at collector
- Number of hose outlets on collector
- Bag capacity
- Type of bag material (traps what micron size of dust particles)
- Drum size
- Cost

Choose a Type

There are three basic types of dust collectors: single-stage, two-stage and cyclone. Each type will collect dust. Aside from design differences, the main considerations for choosing which type to use are number of machines and amount of dust and debris created, length of ductwork, ease of removing captured waste from bags or barrels, noise level and cost.

SINGLE-STAGE DUST COLLECTORS Single-stage collectors are characterized by having two or four filter bags. The bottom bags collect larger debris, and the top bags filter the finer dust and return air back into the workshop. This type is usually the most affordable dust collector in the marketplace. There are two common drawbacks to the single-stage collector, both of which are easily remedied. It is often stated that, because the debris travels directly through the impeller housing, there is unnecessary wear on parts. I have used this style with four bags for over 12 years and have never had mechanical problems. However, I strongly recommend that no

The table saw has a portable dust collector hookup. Jon Magill plans on replacing this stiff hose with a more flexible type. He works with one machine at a time and isn't bothered by moving the dust collector to another machine when changing operations.

large wood fragments or cutoff pieces be vacuumed into the impeller—that would probably cause damage. I don't have a floor sweep, a floor-level debris pickup attachment, connected to the system because I don't want large, heavy objects zooming through the ductwork and slamming into the spinning impeller. However, an in-line separator can be installed in front of the collector to separate out larger debris. This unit settles out the larger debris via baffles, so that only small debris and dust continue through to the impeller and into the filter bags. I think that the second drawback, fine dust exiting the filter bags, is a more serious problem. The filter bags that

come with most collectors are porous enough to allow fine dust through the weave. As a consequence, larger debris is caught in the bags and fine dust migrates throughout the workshop, creating unnecessary (and unpleasant) air pollution. Replacement filter bags that filter down to one micron particle size are recommended.

TWO-STAGE DUST COLLECTORS Two-stage collectors are characterized by a blower motor on top of a collector drum (35 or 50 gallon) and a side-mounted filter bag. These units are designed so that larger debris settles into the drum, and fine dust is captured in the filter bag. The significant drawback to

this type is that the motor housing is heavy and has to be lifted off in order to empty the collector drum (which is also heavy when it's full). Those that use this type often use ropes and pulleys to raise the housing off the drum.

CYCLONIC DUST COLLECTORS A Cyclone collector appears to be industrial; it's a tall steel cylinder with a funneled midsection and a 35 or 50 gallon collector drum. Debris enters the upper chamber and is cyclonically separated. Larger debris spirals downward into the collection drum, and the fine dust is caught in a filter housed within the upper chamber. Very often another series of long and thin filter bags are separate from the cyclone. These filters, called *shaker bags*, further filter the exiting air. Interestingly, there are now two types of cyclone systems: commercially made units and do-it-yourself units (*Wood Magazine*, issue 100, November, 1997).

Using Separators

Separators are becoming more common, and this attachment effectively makes a single-stage collector into a two-stage collector. The inexpensive units look something like an enlarged trash can lid. They are designed with two open ports, one for attaching a dust collection hose from the machine and the other for attach-

The filter bag system for the cyclone dust collector.

ing a hose to the dust collector. The separator, placed on a trash can, then separates heavier chips from lighter dust; that is, chips and dust are drawn from the machine into the separator, where the heavier chips are diverted by a baffle and settle into the trash can, while the lighter dust continues on to the dust collector. These are very useful units, in that they reduce wear on collector impellers and assist in workshop cleanup.

Stay Within Code

Check local building codes concerning the placement of collectors. Certain types of collectors may need to be located outside of the main workshop.

Lay Out Your System

Draw a layout for your woodshop. Locate the collector so that it's out of the way without requiring unnecessary duct lengths. As a reference, consider the vein pattern in a leaf. Determine the length of duct, the number of fittings (elbows, etc.), and the diameter of the duct. Note that the length of the duct and its internal smoothness, and the shape of and number of fittings, all increase frictional resistance to air flow. Any internal friction and/or air turbulence decreases collection efficiency.

Ducts and fittings that have gradual directional changes will help make a system more efficient. Avoid duct runs having abrupt angles or turns. If possible, avoid using 90° T fittings; instead, use 45° Ts to minimize turbulence. If ducts of different diameters are required, use tapered connectors for smoother transitions between the ducts.

Companies such as Air Handling Systems by Manufacturers Service Co., Delta Machinery Corp. and Oneida Air Systems, Inc., provide excellent information regarding how to determine CFM for the system, duct air velocity, system resistance and the proper size of ducts and fittings.

Consider Your Needs

The diameter of the duct will affect air flow. Wood dust requires a minimum velocity of 3500 FPM within the main duct, or debris can settle out of the airstream, leading to blockage problems. The two variables that relate to duct diameter are velocity and static pressure. Larger diameter duct increases static pressure and reduces air velocity; as duct diameter decreases, static pressure decreases and air velocity increases. The main consideration is to minimize static pressure loss. To accomplish that you must must measure each duct run; that is, the length from the machine to the collector. Also, each fitting causes a reduction in air velocity, so fittings must also be factored into the length measurement. The common practice is to assign an "equivalent length" for a fitting. For example, a 90° elbow is equivalent to six feet of duct; a 45° elbow is equivalent to three feet of duct. Therefore, a duct run that consists of 20' of straight 4' duct, three 90° elbows and one 45° elbow is equivalent to 41' of duct.

Now, to use the value, there is another step to calculate the actual static pressure for the duct run. Static pressure is usually based upon 100' of duct. Four-inch- and five-inch-diameter ducts are the most commonly used sizes.

For the example of 41 feet, multiply 0.41 (41' of 100') by 5.5, equaling 2.55" of static pressure ("inches of water"). If the filter bags are dirty, an additional static pressure loss should also be added to the value. As a generalization, add a value of 1, thus equaling 3.55". **Note:** This is for one duct run without any branch runs. If several machines are hooked up to the collector, but are operated one at a time, the duct diameter will be dependent on the machine with the greatest CFM requirement. If you are creating a complicated network of ductwork and fittings, careful calculations of duct length and all fittings is required. Determine the static pressure value for the entire system and compare that value with those of the various dust collectors in the marketplace. This value isn't absolute: A number of factors influence the actual rating. Air leaks, duct crimps and rivets, duct interior smoothness, corrugated flex-hose, dirty filter bags and machine hookup attachments are only a few of the variables influencing dust collector efficiency.

Use Metal Ductwork

Metal duct is slightly more difficult to install than plastic (PVC) pipe, but it is easier to ground it against static electricity. The common method for grounding plastic pipe is to run a ground wire inside the entire length of the pipe and then attach it at either end to the machine and the earth ground. The disadvantage of this method is that wood debris can break the internal wire, unbeknownst to the operator. And debris can lodge around the wire and eventually cause a blockage. I won't use plastic pipe because static electrical charges build up as dust travels rapidly through it—and air-

TYPICAL AIR FLOW REQUIREMENTS
FOR VARIOUS MACHINES

Machine	CFM
Table saw	300–350
Band saw	400–700
Disc sander	300–350
Jointer	350–440
Planer	400–785
Shaper	300–1400
Lathe	350–500

CFM REQUIREMENTS FOR DUCT DIAMETERS

Duct Diameter	CFM@3500 FPM
3"	170
4"	300
5"	475

Duct Diameter	Inches of Static Pressure*
3"	7.5
4"	5.5
5"	4.2
6"	3.5

*3500 FPM per 100' of duct

borne dust has the potential to be highly combustible. I talked with one woodworker who thought he had done all the correct hookups and groundings for using plastic pipe. Yet, late one night, when no one was using the workshop, there was a static discharge within the pipe, and his workshop was lost to fire.

PLASTIC DUCT GUIDELINES If you are determined to use plastic pipe for dust collection because "Old George down the street uses it" or because "Everyone in my woodworkers' club uses it," you should at least do the following:

1. Ground the pipe by installing a taut ground wire inside of it.

2. Also ground the plastic pipe by wrapping a ground wire spirally around the outside of it. Both types of grounding should be done to all pipes in the system, and the wires should be properly attached at either end to machines and a proper ground location.

3. Assemble the plastic pipes so that they can be unassembled for cleaning out chip blockages (use pipe connectors and duct tape).

4. Occasionally check for any internal blockage and for continuity in the internal ground wire. (Look for chip buildup around the wire and for wire abrasion.)

AIR FILTRATION

Air filtration is perhaps one of the most important features that relates to a woodworker's health. Fine dust particles will stay in air suspension for hours. These particles are so small that they are almost invisible. However, a person in the workshop will breathe these particles into the nasal and throat passages and lungs. There is much evidence as to the health risks of breathing dust, so the ideal workshop should have a method of removing these particles. As a doctor woodworking friend once said, "You don't breathe the large chips that settle out on the floor, you breathe the tiny airborne particles that you can't see."

I had several woodworkers tell me that they think their workshops got dustier *after* they installed dust collectors. The first step is to make the dust collection system free of dust leakage. This leakage occurs at both the machine and the filter bags. Well-fit hookups at the machine are mandatory. If the machine's factory-made hookup seems inadequate, make your own. Second, most dust collection bags are susceptible to dust migrating through the fibrous weavings. Most bags capture dust sizes of 10 to 50 microns; smaller sizes escape back into the workshop environment. The best solution is to check with the dust collector

manufacturer about replacing the bags with high-efficiency filter bags, which will filter particles down to 1 micron in size.

Air filtration units are also becoming popular. These units are hung from the ceiling in the room's air circulation pattern, and then they filter the air. By using a continuous-duty fan and a series of filters, very fine airborne dust (1 to 5 microns) is trapped and clean air is circulated back into the workshop. Commercially made units cost $250 to $700. However, it's fairly easy to make your own air filtration unit by building a plywood box and installing a furnace-type fan with several high-quality slide-in furnace-type filters.

The ideal solution for dust collection, especially if your workshop is attached to your house, is to have an efficient unit that is both quiet and powerful enough for use with several machines operating. Suspend metal ductwork from the the ceiling and make certain that the ducts are properly sealed, free of leaks and properly grounded against static electricity buildup. Also, the hookup fittings should be well made and fit tightly on the machines. The dust collector should have high-efficiency filter bags and a manageable system for removing the drums or bags when they are filled. Finally, an air filtration unit should be hung from the ceiling so that fine dust is also captured. If that doesn't make a dust-free woodshop, open a window and the door.

A TYPICAL DUST COLLECTION SYSTEM

The most confusing aspect of setting up a dust collection system is understanding the relationships of air volume or CFM (air measured in cubic feet per minute) and static pressure (the resistance to air at rest in a duct) to the length and diameter of duct and the number of machines in the workshop.

Let's assume that your workshop is in either a garage or a basement, and you are the only person operating machinery. The goal is to connect the dust collection system to a table saw, band saw, jointer, planer, disc/belt sander, lathe and drill press.

1. After you have reviewed the specifications of all dust collectors, select the one that has the greatest horsepower (at least 1½ to 3 hp) and is rated greater than 700 CFM at 5" to 6" of static pressure. For example:

- Grizzly Model G1029 2 hp, 1182 CFM at 5.00" of static pressure
- Oneida Air Blower 2 hp, 900 CFM at 8.00" of static pressure
- Delta Model 50-1812 hp, 1100 CFM at 8.50" of static

pressure
- Bridgewood BW-0033 hp, 1950 CFM at 5.80" of static pressure
- Oneida Air Blower 3 hp, 1350 CFM at 8.00" of static pressure

2. Determine the filter bag area. Typical bag sizes range from 10 to 40 square foot. As a guide, have at least 1 square foot of filter bag area for every 10 CFM. For example, a 10 square feet filter bag is useful for a 1000 CFM collector. If the filter bag area is less than the rated CFM, install larger bags.

3. Install a metal 6" and 5" main duct from the collector. Generally, 6"-diameter duct is used nearest the collector and then it's reduced to a 5"-diameter duct further from the collector.

4. Please don't use plastic pipes. Plastic pipe can be dangerous because of the significant static electricity charges that are generated when wood dust and chips travel through the pipes.

5. Securely assemble the duct system. Assemble the duct system with pop rivets, sheet metal screws or duct tape. Seal all ductwork with silicone sealer and be sure there are no small openings or cracks, which cause air loss.

6. Minimize the use of elbows

and turns. Use large-radius elbows when branching off of the main duct to the individual machines; don't use 90° T fittings. Also, use 45° Y fittings for any turns off of the main duct line. If it's necessary to use a smaller diameter hose, use reducer fittings on the machine side of the elbows. Use metal ductwork up to within approximately three feet of machine. Then use flexible hose as the 3' connector to the machine. Properly ground the flexible hose by wrapping the ground wire around the hose and attaching one end to the metal duct and the other to the ground.

7. Use gates (blast gates) at all machines to control air to each machine. Place the gate between the metal duct and the flexible hose.

8. When using the dust collection system, keep blast gates closed at unused machines.

9. If the dust collector is in an out-of-the way location, install a remote control device for wireless on/off operation. These units are available from most sellers of dust collectors.

CONSIDER WOOD TOXICITY

Perhaps, after the discussion of machines and collectors, there is

A PARTIAL LISTING OF WOODS AND THEIR POTENTIAL HAZARDS

Wood	Reaction Location*
Arborvitae	respiratory system
Bald Cypress	respiratory system
Balsam Fir	skin, eyes
Beech	respiratory system, skin, eyes
Birch	respiratory system
Black Locust	skin, eyes
Blackwood	skin, eyes
Boxwood	respiratory system, skin, eyes
Cashew	skin, eyes
Cedar, Western Red	respiratory system, skin, eyes
Cocobolo	respiratory system, skin, eyes
Ebony	respiratory system, skin, eyes
Elm	skin, eyes
Goncalo Alves	skin, eyes
Greenheart	respiratory system, skin, eyes
Hemlock	respiratory system
Mahogany, African	respiratory system, skin, eyes
Mahogany, American	skin, eyes
Mansonia	respiratory system, skin, eyes
Maple, Spalted	respiratory system
Myrtle	respiratory system
Oak	skin, eyes
Obeche	respiratory system, skin, eyes
Oleander	respiratory system, skin, eyes
Olivewood	respiratory system, skin, eyes
Padauk	respiratory system, skin, eyes
Pau Ferro	skin, eyes
Purpleheart	nausea, malaise
Redwood, Sequoia	respiratory system, skin, eyes
Rosewood, Brazilian	respiratory system, skin, eyes
Rosewood, East Indian	respiratory system, skin, eyes
Satinwood	respiratory system, skin, eyes
Sassafras	nausea, malaise
Snakewood	respiratory system
Spruce	respiratory system
Teak	respiratory system, skin, eyes
Walnut, Black	skin, eyes
Wenge	respiratory system, skin, eyes
Willow	respiratory system, nausea, malaise
Yew	nausea, malaise, cardiac
Zebrawood	skin, eyes

*This does not represent the order in which any ailments or problems occur.
This information on wood toxicity has been taken from:
Stanley N. Wellborn, "Health Hazards in Woodworking," *Fine Woodworking* (Winter 1977);
American Woodturner (June 1990).

one other topic that needs to be mentioned—toxic woods. Although dust collectors will remove the majority of dust and chips, their purpose isn't just to make a tidy workshop. You also want to remove physical threats to your health and well-being.

Sometimes I think that working with wood is like having a tiger for a pet—it looks great but it can bite your hand off. While everyone has different sensitivity levels, wood is known to cause skin and eye allergies, as well as respiratory and cardiac problems. Some woods are classified as *primary irritants* because they are highly toxic (West Indian satinwood, for example). Other woods are classified as *sensitizers* because they may cause physical reactions after repeated exposures (such as cocobolo).

One of the toxic conditions that is often difficult, if not impossible, for consumers to know about is wood contaminated with pesticides and preservatives. Treated lumber in the United States is labeled as such, and the manufacturers post handling guidelines for their products. Unfortunately, while there are many chemicals banned from use in the United States, those chemicals are often used by foreign companies.

If you have questions about wood toxicity, consult your physician, the National Institute of

Occupational Safety and Health (OSHA), your local city health department, and/or textbooks on poisonous plants.

Wood toxicity isn't solved just by using a dust collector and an air filtration system. Although these systems will certainly remove most dust and chips, there is still fine dust circulating within the workshop. If you are concerned about residual dust (or dust made unrelated to dust collection), there are several options.

Safety Guidelines

- Always wear some form of face mask or respirator. Disposable masks are often form-fit around the nose and mouth; reusable respirators have replaceable filter cartridges. If these are inadequate for your needs, there are space-age-looking air purifying respirators. These have a hard hat with a clear plastic face shield. The shield form fits the entire face, and at the back of the hard hat is a fan unit that blows filtered air over the top of the head and down across the face. Note that you are breathing filtered air—and not breathing through a filter. While these units are expensive, they offer features not found in standard filter masks, such as full-face protection from flying debris (they are popular with lathe turners) and comfort for woodworkers with beards or eyeglasses (standard filter masks and respirators don't fit well on beards and under eyeglasses).

- Wear long-sleeved shirts to keep dust off of your arms. Don't wear loose or unbuttoned shirts, because loose clothes and machinery are a disaster waiting to happen. Long-sleeved T-shirts are a better choice.

- If you are sanding, create air circulation *away* from the work area. Place a portable fan at one end of the workbench and sand at the other end. The fan should blow dust away from you.

9

INVESTING IN A GREAT WORKBENCH

The workbench is a tool. It's OK to make it attractive, but also make it useful—and don't be nervous about nicks.

THE WORKBENCH IS A TOOL

The workbench is the universal tool found in any type of workshop. It's difficult to imagine any type of woodwork being done without some sort of table-height flat work area. Even if we divide woodworking into two camps, power tool users and non-power tool users, there is still agreement that the workbench is a necessity. However, the type of workbench used is very much open to discussion. After all, workbenches have been used for thousands of years, which makes for more than a few workbench designs to consider. The workbench may be nothing more than a bench top supported against a garage wall, or it may be a reproduction of a Shaker workbench. Quite possibly because of the historical nature of woodworking, the workbench is one of those tools that is evaluated or designed with a reference to the concept of *traditional*. Because of the popularity and availability of information concerning woodworking, almost every historical workbench can be, and

Close-up of antique workbench in Tom Dailey's workshop.

has been, recreated; ancient Roman, Japanese, Chinese, medieval English, French, German and Early American, to name a few.

Having said that the well of information is rather deep, I would like to focus on the workbench that might function best in today's workshop. What confuses the issue of workbench design is the very enrichment that makes the workbench desirable. Just what is the *ideal* workbench, or does such a thing actually exist? Are we blessed or cursed by the historical workbench? Does the modern woodworker actually have access to modern workbench theories and designs? Are the advocates of traditional woodworking ignoring the obvious, and are the power tool users missing the beauty and function of a traditional workbench?

Bench Basics

The stereotypical workbench is about 3'-wide and 6'-long, and has side- and front-mounted vises and a reasonably flat work surface. This workbench probably has some sort of storage, either below the bench top or in a tool tray or rack behind the top's back edge. This stereotype workbench is well made, and has a thick laminated hardwood top, stout legs and is very heavy. Some workbenches are so heavy that it takes four people to lift and move them. If this workbench is traditionally designed, it has a row of holes accompanying the end vise. These holes are there to secure bench stops (short pieces of wood or steel) so that a board can be held fast between the vise and the bench stops. Generally, this type of workbench was designed and

built for use with hand tools, principally bench planes, hand saws and chisels. The other major physical feature is bench height. And this is a function of the relationship between the woodworker's height and the height of a board to be worked, both on the surface and on the edge. If a bench is either too high or too low, the woodworker can't maximize body comfort and strength, and the work process will be compromised. If the bench is too lightweight, the planing action will cause the bench to rack diagonally or skip around the floor.

If one studies the workbenches of the time just before the proliferation of electric tools in the United States, it's very noticeable that workbenches were rather utilitarian looking. They had large surfaces, a tail vise and front vise and some device for

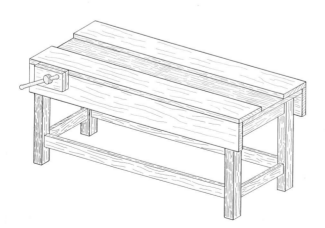

Old-style carpenter's workbench that features front vise and top surface with two levels. Center section can hold tools and small objects.

Traditionally designed workbench with wooden vises, square bench-dog holes and open understructure.

supporting long boards. Many of the benches appear to be constructed of thick, wide boards with an open-leg housing. Of course, there were exceptions to the open-leg design, and there were benches with storage areas. However, tools were generally stored in tool chests kept near the workbench.

Few of us now store tools in large tool chests that look like steamer trunks. Today's woodworker prefers to build large wall cabinets, or multiple wall cabinets, for storage. We now prefer to design workbenches so that there is some storage under the bench top. Having smaller workshops does require the full utilization of all spaces; the additional bench structure and weight of the stored tools helps to make a strong and heavy workbench, thus reducing vibrations and bench movement when it's used.

DESIGNING A WORKBENCH

The real question about workbench design is: How will the workbench be used? Nostalgia aside, that revered turn-of-the-century workbench was used for long hours of work and commerce. Someone stood at that bench for many hours a day and made things with hand tools. That tool chest was filled with assorted hand planes, moulding planes, braces, auger bits and so

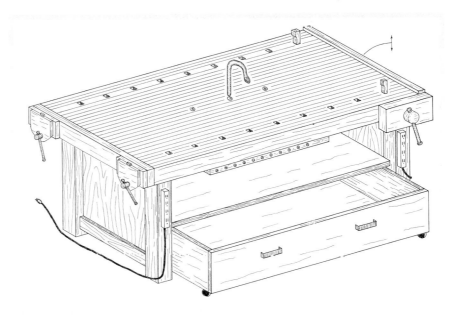

Concept workbench. It features two rows of bench-stop holes, two end vises, one front vise, storage shelf, rollout storage container, electrical boxes on front legs, adjustable edge stop and bench hook in center of work top.

forth. These chests were frequently so filled with tools that one description of them might be "crammed orderliness." Often, hundreds of tools were nestled within a maze of special boxes, drawers, containers and holders. Also, the lumber used was large and heavy, and rough boards were often hand planed and hand sawed. This was state-of-the-art equipment, as well as the work style for that time. Is that how the modern woodworker now works? If so, then there are many historical texts available that will help to recreate that type of workbench. If, however, you are using electric tools and working with plywood, perhaps a different workbench design is in order.

This isn't about not using

hand tools or bashing traditional tools. Instead, it's important to design the workbench so that its function matches today's needs. Although it's very possible to own and drive an antique car, it doesn't make sense to use that car for stop- (mostly) and-go rush-hour driving. The same applies for the workbench. If we use the traditional workbench for modern work, perhaps we are creating an unnecessary struggle. Generally, hand tools are now secondary processing tools and are mostly used for detail work, such as trimming, cutting joints or planing an edge. The primary processing tools are the table saw, compound miter saw, radial arm saw, band saw, jointer and planer. Furthermore, the principal tools that aid in refining boards into objects are routers, drills, sanders, scroll saws and biscuit joiners. The old fellows of the past didn't have plywood, particleboard, MDF and other 4' × 8' sheet goods to work. Plywood and other related manmade materials, besides being heavy and awkward to move, aren't made to be cut, shaped or prepared with hand tools.

The issue is that we now use an assortment of hand and power tools and materials requiring workbench performance far different than that of 1849 or 1905. If you're building a workbench for the first time, this might be the time to reassess the typical workbench design and build one from a fresh perspective.

Design Considerations

- Workbench height
- Material used for bench top
- Surface area required for accommodating materials
- Size and shape of workbench relative to the type of work and tools
- Movable or not
- Free-standing or against wall
- Holding system(s) for:
  routing
  drilling
  belt sanding
  finish sanding
  carving
  hand tool use (i.e., planes and saws)
- Use of clamps on the workbench

- Tool storage
- Electrical hookup
- Vises:
  front
  side
  specialty
- Make single, special or multipurpose benches

Workbench Height

Bench height is one of the most important dimensional features to consider. The proper height will allow the user to work comfortably and to efficiently use tools. Improper bench height leads to stooping over, sore back and neck muscles and awkward arm movements. I once was instructing a class on using hand planes and a student showed me a board edge that he had just finished. I sighted down the foot-long board and was very impressed. There wasn't one place on the edge that was square to the board's surface. In fact, the board was reminiscent of a Mobius strip. Not wanting to hurt his feelings, I asked him to demonstrate his planing technique for me. What became obvious was that the work surface was too high, and the strange edge was a result of his unnatural reach to the board and the change of his body position as he moved down the board's edge.

There are several popular heights for general-purpose workbenches. Most commer-

cially-made workbenches are usually 33" to 36" in height. Of course, it would be impossible for manufacturers to offer an infinite variety of bench heights. Therefore, if you want this type of workbench, it would be best to purchase either the correct height bench or one slightly lower. It's much easier to place blocks under the legs to raise the bench than it is to cut the legs and make the bench shorter. I'm 6'1" and my workbench is 35" in height. I'm not sure that's an ideal height for others, but for me it's comfortable.

To determine the height for a workbench, you must first determine the height from the floor to the top of the work you are doing. For example, a 1" × 10"-wide board is to be edge planed. If the board is clamped in a position so that the edge is up, the edge height is then approximately 43" from the floor. This was computed by assuming a 35"-high workbench and that the board has 2" of width in a front vise. Now, if that same board needs surface work, the floor-to-work surface height is 36". If you are comfortable working within the 36" to 43" range, 35" is a good bench height.

First, prioritize the tools that you will use the most at the workbench. Make a list of the tools that you will use, from the most use to the least. For a hypothetical example, the most used to least used workbench tools might be a router, belt sander, chisels, hand planes and hand saws. Now, make a best guess as to the height above the bench top at which these tools would be used. Generally, the router, belt sander and chisels will be used on flat stock (¼" to 4" in height), and hand planes will be used mostly on edges (¼" to 24" in height). You may want to make mock-ups of various heights and pantomime the motions involved in using belt sanders, routers and hand planes. Since there is no perfect height, pick a height that seems to average out the various work heights from this pantomime effort. Have someone else watch you doing the pantomime to find out if you unconsciously stoop over while working. Surprisingly, this is common, and you may find that at certain heights you keep a straight back and are also comfortable in this position. You might find that the generic 33" to 36" heights are

fine, or you may find that 30" or 38" is more comfortable for you. Woodworkers don't come in one size, and there is no reason to assume that workbenches should either.

There is one other situation in which bench height is critical. There are a number of jigs and fixtures that are useful for specialized work, including such things as the Leigh Dovetail Jig or a shop-made tenoning jig. If the jig is clamped to the workbench, the workpieces must be shorter than the distance to the floor. There are two solutions: Dig a hole in the floor for the longer boards, or raise the jig above the workbench. Since the hole option isn't reasonable, many woodworkers have built higher benches for this function. Do not operate a router at a raised bench in a way that your face is in line with the cutting action: This is *very* dangerous. Nor should you use a movable step stool or ladder to reach the jig. The best method is to build a box that's 3" to 10" in height, at-

tach the jig to it and then clamp the entire assembly to the workbench.

If I had the space I would have two workbenches. One bench would be at a standard height and would be used for joinery, clamping and general-purpose use. The other bench would be approximately 18" to 28" in height, and it would be used for placing chairs, chests and other furniture pieces on for assembly, detail work and finishing. When detailing or finishing a piece that is either sitting on the floor or up on the standard bench, it always seems to have a wrong visual perspective, or the piece is in an awkward, hard-to-reach position. A lower bench makes it easier to see and move the piece.

Bench-Top Materials

Is a laminated maple bench top better than one of 2 × 4s and MDF (medium-density fiberboard)? The maple top certainly looks better, but does it add to the

Low, mobile workstation. Features drawers on both sides of unit and wheels. Lockable wheels are recommended. Unit is approximately 16" to 24" in height.

Low workstations are perfect for work projects that are too tall for a standard workbench.

functionality of the bench? Traditional workbenches are usually made of hardwoods such as maple, beech, or oak, but these benches were developed when natural wood was the only material choice. Much can be said about the natural beauty of wood benches, a beauty that is enhanced by the patina of age and use. When you are making fine woodworking pieces, it seems almost natural to visually connect a beautiful bench with the workpiece. There is the old adage that you should use your best tools when attempting your best work. Perhaps the luster and charm of a seasoned hardwood bench do help motivate a woodworker toward a higher level of work. A hardwood bench that has dovetail and mortise-and-

tenon joints is a constant reminder of the best of woodworking and craftsmanship. The hardwood bench top does have features beyond beauty. A 2"- or 3"-thick bench top is ideal for work that requires the pounding of a mallet or hammer. The top's thickness and density offer a solidity that minimizes tool recoil, bounce-back and workpiece stability. The sheer weight of a solid wood bench top also provides stability and stiffness, which means that heavy materials and projects won't distort the top. And hardwood tops are easy to maintain. As the top wears or even distorts, it can be reflattened with hand planes or belt sanders.

But there are other considerations regarding laminated work-

bench tops. The principal drawbacks to a laminated top are that they are expensive and difficult to make. There are approximately 54 board feet of wood in a 3"×36"×72" bench top. Add on an additional 20 percent for waste and that's about 65 board feet to purchase. Call a local lumberyard and get a quote of the current price of maple, cherry and oak.

When preparing wood for a bench top, each lamination surface must be planed very flat. Then the entire lamination assembly must be carefully aligned when it is glued so that it will remain very flat during and after gluing. Any twists that occur during glue-up will result in a piece requiring difficult work to make it flat. Other factors to consider: A laminated top is heavy and awkward to move, and when it's being glued up, heavy-duty bar clamps spaced about 6" apart on either side of the workpiece are also required. Someone once said that you need a workbench in order to build a workbench. That's very true when dealing with the gluing-up process. A workbench is flat and therefore the ideal surface on which to rest the clamped-up workpiece. If you plan on using a garage floor as a resting surface for the glued assembly, can you be certain that the floor is flat? If it isn't, the uneven floor will introduce twists to the clamped workpiece.

I've noticed that many more woodworkers are now building bench tops with man-made materials. Part of the reason for this is that it's easier to construct the top with sheet materials. A frame is built first, and then one or more layers are added. Often the top layer is attached with screws so that it can be replaced when it's worn. The principal materials used are MDF, tempered hardboard and particleboard. Solid-wood edges are attached to the top so that the sheet materials are contained and don't break or crumble.

It's easier to build a 3′ × 8′ top of these materials than to build one of hardwood. There is enough material in two 4′ × 8′ sheets for a 2¼″ × 32″ × 96″ top (two 32″ and two 16″ strips). The compromise necessary when using man-made materials is that the top isn't as dense or resilient as hardwoods. However, flatness is easier to attain, and the top can be replaced or repaired easily. I've also noticed that some woodworkers pencil-sketch directly onto particleboard tops. Some actually draw, with a T-square and triangles, full-size drawings of their current projects. When that project is completed, the drawings are erased and the surface is ready for the next one.

SURFACE AREA REQUIRED FOR MATERIALS

It may seem obvious that a workbench holds stuff on the top surface, but when one is working on a project with stacks of wood, and there are odds and ends of wood, assorted tools, power cords, glue bottles and so on, the top of the bench gets cluttered rapidly and the bench seems small. I suppose the cliche, what-ever size you have will always fill up, applies. So the solution is to build the largest bench possible. A large bench isn't just for building large projects. Actually, the workbench is the only open flat area in a woodshop that isn't flooring or doesn't have a blade projecting out of it. The bench then becomes the focal point and command center for everything from stirring paints to sorting screws. Rarely is my workbench empty. And when I use it for sorting wood for a project or to stack furniture parts, some part of the bench is still filled with assorted tools and notebooks.

When I read books about the Shakers and their workshops, what I see are beautiful, clean and empty workbenches—and I wonder what those large surface benches looked like when they were being used. I imagine stacks of wood, assorted tools,

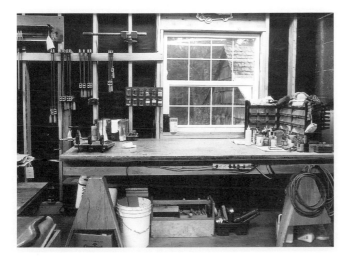

Doug Matthews likes having portable workstations for his antique restoration business. This workstation is used much like a typical workbench.

This portable workstation is used as a glue drying location for repaired antiques.

boxes of hardware and cans of finishes everywhere on that bench. I appreciate that the Shakers placed great value in neatness and cleanliness, but I do believe that during work, those large workbenches were covered with stuff.

Free-Standing or Against a Wall

Workbench location is simple: Place it against a wall or let it stand in the workshop so that you can walk completely around it. If space is at a premium, place the bench against a wall. This reduces some uses, such as placing long boards and clamps across the bench and using all four edges for clamping. However, the workbench will be more stable when it's attached to a wall, and the wall above the workbench usually becomes a storage area for commonly used tools.

Free-standing workbenches can be left at one location or moved as necessary. I appreciate the free-standing workbench because I can position long bar clamps across the bench when gluing, and because I can work completely around an object on the bench. Not having to move an object is especially useful when repairing antiques or applying finishes. Tool storage is further away with this type of bench, but it's not that much of a distance and generally isn't a problem.

If you need a work surface in a garage and would like to have the floor area unobstructed by table legs, attach diagonal braces to wall studs.

Small bench-top tools are neatly arranged on this functional workstation in Dean Bershaw's workshop.

Shape of Workbench

Another stereotype of workbench design is the rectangular bench—22″ × 72″, 24″ × 78″, 30″ × 66″, etc. Generally, this shape is comfortable for most hand tool work; however, when coupled with the traditional two vises, this shape doesn't always lend itself to power tool use. End vise and bench stops were designed to secure a board when using planes and chisels. The vise stop and bench-top stop usually are about ¾″ wide, and the board is pinched between the two. When you study most traditional workbenches, it becomes clear that the design emphasis is the bench-stop system, and these benches were designed to secure more or less narrow boards. Traditional workbenches are definitely pre-electric and preplywood.

A description of a working-condition scenario is in order to picture limitations. Suppose a 24″ square of plywood requires a rabbet on all four edges. If the bench stops are used, the router with fence and bit can only cut one edge at a time, and therefore the board will have to be unclamped and reclamped three more times, because you cannot continuously cut all four edges in one pass. Most likely the router fence won't clear the bench top, and the two bench stops are also obstructions. Of course, this four-

edge rabbet can be cut on the router table, but there are times when the workbench offers easier setup, except for the bench stops. Another common problem with the bench stop and end vise occurs when belt sanding. The nature of a belt sander is that the belt turns so that, when it's running, the belt pulls the workpiece toward its back end and the operator. Since the workpiece is pulled in one direction, it's a common practice to place the workpiece against a bench stop and sand. This works reasonably well, except when the workpiece is wider than a few inches. When the belt sander is aligned to the bench stop, it pulls squarely against the stop. If the sander is at one side or the other of the board, it will cause the board to pivot against the stop, making sanding nearly impossible. The traditional solution to this is to use both bench stops to secure the workpiece. If, however, there are numerous workpieces of assorted lengths, the operator will constantly be moving bench stops to different bench holes and tightening, loosening and re-tightening the vise. This makes for slow work, especially when using a fast and powerful power tool like the belt sander. Another solution is to clamp a long strip of wood in the end vise so that the entire width of the workpiece is touching it. This reduces the

pivoting motion and makes sanding much easier and quicker. However, many of the traditional end vises aren't designed for this type of clamping. And some traditional workbenches that have rear-mounted tool trays also have narrow flat areas, and these two features make it difficult to secure wider workpieces. If the workbench is against a wall, wider workpieces may not have sufficient space for safe and easy work.

Considering these operations is critical to designing a workbench. If you know the type of work that will be done, the workbench can be configured accordingly. There are definite work conditions relative to the type of material being used for projects. A stack of plywood pieces could actually tip over some lightweight benches, or a workbench shape might make it difficult to work on certain constructions. The general shape of the workbench will affect more than workshop area square footage. It will affect the ease of positioning work projects, tool use, tool storage and operator maneuverability. I'm not a fan of the traditional Scandinavian bench, which has an L-shaped wing projecting from the edge. Part of this dislike is because I'm left-handed—and the benches I've used aren't. But more importantly, I really don't like that front projection. I realize that there are hand tool advocates that like this design, but for me, it's awkward to use and easy to bump into when walking by the bench. I see no reason to have the clamping/holding projection for hand tool use.

Movable or Not?

Smaller workshops often require machine mobility. More machines are being mounted on mobile bases than ever before. Mobile bases permit the woodworker to move very heavy machines from storage to an area of use and then return the machine to storage. Mobile-base frames have locking wheels so that the machine can be used safely. Generally, workbenches aren't considered mobile objects. However, a few years ago, table saws and jointers were thought of only as *stationary* machines. I would suggest that if a workbench is made mobile, a retractable mechanism should be used for the locked position. This allows the workbench to be moved, but when it's in position, the bench legs would be in direct contact with the floor. If the workbench is in some sort of carriage that has locking wheels, the legs aren't directly touching the floor. Aside from mobility, it's necessary to avoid micromovement in the bench once it's in position. If the floor's uneven, shims are eas-

ily tapped under the legs. However, workbenches that are in carriages will have micromovements that are annoying and bothersome when you are trying to do fine detail work. Solid contact with the floor is best. One possible solution is to make wheel systems for each leg set that flip up out of the way once the bench is in position.

Another alternative is to have movable workstations. This system works well when the workshop is also used to store automobiles (some people call these rooms "garages"). Sawhorses (commercially available folding sawhorses are ideal) are set in position, the work surface is secured and tools are then attached to the workstation.

Holding Systems for the Bench

Is there anything in the workshop that's a single-function object universal enough to encompass all woodworking needs? Can you do work with only one drill bit size, one chisel, or one grit of sandpaper? If you can manage this feat, I'm impressed. The very nature of woodworking is one of increments and subtle adjustments. Rough-sawing a piece is the opposite of fine-tuning. The very nature of a woodshop is the variety of tools and machines that are used between these two extremes.

If this point of view is accu-

rate, why should we assume that a workbench should have only one or two methods of securing workpieces? Does the traditional bench-vise and bench-stop system perform adequately for cabinetmakers, lathe turners, carvers, antique restorers, picture frame makers and miniaturists? Or, should we consider that function should be the measure of bench design? I know that I've modified my workbench to accommodate router and belt sander use and the periodic woodcarving that I do. And that's the heart of this issue. Define your most frequently performed tasks and develop specialized holding systems for those tasks. Standard-issue holding systems might get you close to the best way of holding something, but efficiency necessitates fine-tuning the holding systems.

The principal purpose of any holding system is to secure the workpiece while work is done. The holding system should be easy to use, it should grip and tightly hold the workpiece and it should store away quickly and efficiently. Complicated holding systems consisting of many parts should be viewed with skepticism. Infrequently used parts and accessories are easily lost, abandoned or forgotten.

Without creating a multitude of diversity, there are a few basic woodworking functions that

Jon Magill's portable workstation for horizontal router table and planer. The commercial sawhorses have a retaining track on their top surface and retain cleats that are mounted on the underside of the work surface.

require specialized workbench holding systems.

- routing
- drilling
- belt sanding
- finish sanding
- carving
- hand tool use (i.e., planes and saws)

Ideally, any workpiece should be secured so that clamps or stops don't interfere with tool use. For example, it's very easy to secure a workpiece to the workbench with a C clamp, except that it's nearly impossible to continuously use the router because the clamp blocks access. The same problem applies to carving. If the workpiece is secured with C clamps, the carver has to be careful not to push the chisel into the clamp, or the clamp has to be constantly moved to reveal carving area.

To avoid this problem when routing and sanding, there are two commercial systems: a foam pad, similar to the padding found under wall-to-wall carpeting, and vacuum vises. Vacuum vises offer incredible holding strength, but they require an air pump motor and an air line, and they are expensive. Vacuum vises might be better suited to commercial woodworking because their efficiency is related to all-day usage and time savings. The foam pads are inexpensive, easily used, easily stored away and replaceable.

The end of the workbench is easily modified to hold different types of board stops. These simple devices are useful for capturing workpieces, and work well for belt sanding or relief carving.

This bench accessory can be further enhanced by the addition of a thin strip located at the other end of the workpiece. This secures the workpiece so that sanding, some routing and other surface work can be done. These strips can be clamped or made to fit bench-dog holes. They also can be shaped to match odd-shaped workpieces.

The router is such a useful tool (it's really nothing more than

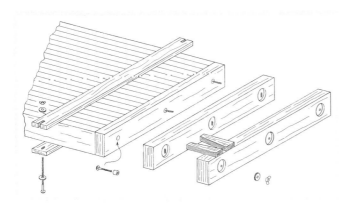

Different edge pieces that can be attached to the end of the workbench. The workbench edge has a cap piece that includes three exposed bolt threads. These bolts are attached through glued dowel sections.

The board (center drawing) has three recessed locations with elongated slots. The bolt threads are through these slots, and the edge board is secured with wing nuts. The edge board can be raised as a catch board at the end of the workbench. This is useful for belt sanding workpieces.

The edge board with two attached wedge-shaped pieces (far right side drawing) is also secured with wing nuts to the three bolt threads. This edge board is useful for securing workpieces when edge planing with hand planes.

Note: There are a number of other edge board design possibilities that can be incorporated onto the end of the workbench.

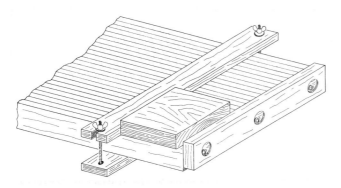

This drawing illustrates how the workpiece is secured with an adjustable edge stop. Also note the use of additional retainer system: two strips of wood secured with wing nuts. Top strip has cutouts so that bolt is easy to position.

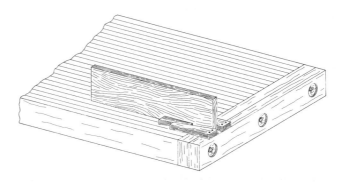

This drawing illustrates how a workpiece is secured with the use of additional wedges.

a high-speed motor with handles!) that a separate workbench dedicated to router use is worth constructing. This workbench should be built higher than a standard bench, approximately 40". This height is determined by holding a router with your elbows bent at 90° and measuring the distance from the floor to the bottom of the router. The bench should be somewhat narrow, approximately 12", and 48" to 60" in length. The narrow width permits router access to either side of a workpiece that is off the bench

top. Also, construction projects, such as a box or a drawer without tops or bottoms, can be slid onto the bench top for work. Attach an end vise with a 12" stop and drill rows of holes along both edges. If you drill round bench-stop holes, bolts with square heads make excellent stops. They will pivot when either a straight or curved workpiece is aligned against them. The base must be constructed so that the router bench won't tip over. Heavy pedestals with broad feet are recommended.

Another useful workbench accessory is the sanding platform. Make the platform box approximately 3" to 6" in height and whatever length and width you choose. It is clamped to the workbench and has a port for attaching a vacuum hose. The top surface is perforated with either slots or holes so that when the vacuum is used, dust is drawn down into the box.

There is so much diversity in woodcarving that there isn't a single holding system for all applications. For some carvers, a heavy-

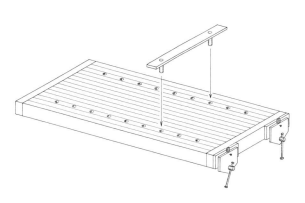

Bench top with two rows of round bench-dog holes and two end vises. Stop board with two dowels that are same diameter as bench-dog holes is used to capture workpiece between it and vises. This is especially useful when using belt sander or router.

Bench top with only a front vise. Stop boards, with both straight and curved edges, can be held in vise and secured on opposite edge with screws. These stops are very useful when using the belt sander. The operator stands at left end of the vise and the workpiece is butted against the stop board. When power sanding, the workpiece is drawn against the stop and secured. If sander is used from the right side, the board will no longer be secured, and an additional stop or clamp is then required.

duty leather glove is adequate. They simply hold a small piece of wood in the gloved hand and carve with the other. Other carvers might use large die grinders to shape a tree stump. This sort of workpiece is heavy and probably requires minimal clamping. Typically, carvers use some sort of screw or lag bolt mounted point up through the workbench top and secured into the base of the workpiece. Another option is power arms. These have movable head plates that are attached to the base of the workpiece. By lever action, the head can be moved so that the workpiece can be worked on at an infinite variety of angles. Generally, power arms are not meant for very heavy workpieces.

Clamps on the Workbench

In most woodshops, floor space is a luxury and the workbench serves multiple purposes. The workbench is the flattest work surface in the workshop and, if it's wide enough, it can be used for clamps when gluing. I use my workbench to support bar clamps up to 4' long for gluing. And, since my bench is 7' long, I can glue up substantial workpieces. The I-beam-style bar clamps are shaped to rest on their clamp fittings, making it easy to set them almost anywhere on the bench top.

Workbench with drawers. Heavy workpiece is held with vise and movable support. The support has holes at different heights.

Another useful clamping situation is being able to secure workpieces anywhere on the workbench with adjustable, deep-throat clamps. If the workbench has drawers, tool trays or other irregular-shaped constructions under the bench top, this usually reduces clamping in that area. I chose to have the bench top edges free of any obstructions so that I could use clamps on all four edges. This permits me, for example, to clamp a workpiece on the back edge and then continue working at the front edge.

Workbench Tool Storage

The ideal tool storage would be that all tools used at the bench are stored within arm's length. Since most workshops are compact, storage is reasonably close. However, there are tools that are used so frequently that some storage at the workbench is necessary. Once again, prioritize your tools and decide on the most important. The typical storage is at the wall behind the workbench, in the workbench itself and on shelves and in cabinets somewhere within the shop.

Many workbenches incorporate a tool well or tool tray that is located either on the back edge or the end of the workbench. And the world seems to be divided into two groups: lovers and haters of tool trays. I'm not fond of them because they always seem to be filled with debris and hand tools that are hidden under other tools. However, my biggest gripe is that tool trays minimize workbench clamping area, and that they create extra bench-top width but no extra top area for supporting wide workpieces such as chair legs. To overcome these shortcomings, instead of a permanently installed tool tray, make a tray that is movable and has a top lid. The tray can then be secured at any location or can be removed altogether. The lid will help keep unwanted debris at bay and will add additional surface area.

First consider several of the limitations of storage near the workbench. Wall storage behind a bench means that storage is useful only if you can reach it. Tools stored 6' from the floor probably can't be reached if you

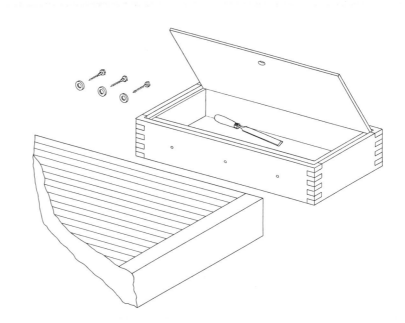

Small tool tray with lid. Tray is attached to the edge of the workbench with lag screws. Lid is useful for two purposes: additional work surface that is flush with bench top, and to keep debris out of tool well.

are standing in front of the bench. Storage underneath a bench top is always subject to being blocked by clamps, workpieces and anything else positioned in front of the bench. The workbench area is space-limited, and there is no need to store tools that are infrequently used. I store a few power tools on a shelf in the workbench, and the majority of items such as power tools, measuring tools, chisels and block planes are two or three steps away in drawers and open cabinets. My personal choice of power tools stored at the workbench is based on frequency of use and the notion that some tools just seem like they belong at the workbench. I have the cordless drill, 4"×24" belt

sander, several finish sanders and a plate joiner all at arm's length. I also store several plastic containers on this shelf. In them I keep an assortment of nails, small screws and washers. Routers and other power tools are about 6' away, and most of the hand tools are about 4' away. The importance of these distances becomes obvious when work is underway. The closer the tools are to the work project, the less frustrating it is. In fact, traveling 6' during some constructions seems like 20'. Someone once said that, given time, anyone can cut dovetails, but to cut good dovetails quickly requires a master craftsman. If the time factor related to finding and selecting tools can be reduced, we take one more step toward better craftsmanship.

Electrical Hookups

We are entering the twenty-first century: Feel free to add electrical outlets to the workbench. I suggest electrical strips attached to the legs as the principal outlets for the workbench, with additional wall outlets at either end of the workbench area. Electrical outlets behind the bench top create the problem of electrical cords running directly over the workbench. This adds to the confusion and clutter, which intensifies during project construction. Additionally, it's dangerous to have electrical cords draped over the work area simply because these cords are too easily cut by sharp cutting tools or operating power tools. Electrical cords that dangle freely to the floor are much safer. Electrical outlets mounted on the front edge or underside are awkward and inconvenient to use, and are often in the way for clamping work.

Outlet strips are really fancy extension cords. For most electrical tools, extension cords of a reasonable length are OK. However, as the amperage increases in the more powerful tools, it's best to carefully read the section of the owner's manual related to extension cords. Some electrical tools come with long power cords, and the additional length of an exten-

sion cord can lead to electrical problems. My belt sander is rated at 10.5 amps, 1220 watts and has a 15' power cord, and it doesn't like extension cords. When I have used an extension cord, the circuit breaker switches off after a few minutes of use.

It's always difficult, and maybe pointless, to state that one tool is more important or more useful than another. However, after working at the workbench for several hours, I always seem to end up with a tangle of power cords attached to various sanders, drills, plate joiners, heat guns and such. Then I use the battery-powered cordless drill. It's probably the most taken for granted, yet wonderful, power tool in the woodshop. These drills are available in a large variety of sizes, shapes, powers and colors. They are powerful enough to drive numerous drywall screws, and the battery can be recharged in less than 30 minutes. And with a keyless chuck, it's quick and easy to change bits and drivers. The cordless drill could be the perfect tool for the woodworker, especially when at the workbench.

Choosing a Vise

Once again, tradition dictates a particular element of workbench design, namely that workbenches have at least two vises. Typically, the front vise is

mounted on the left front and the shoulder vise is mounted on the left edge. If you are left-handed, reverse that pattern for the proper left-handed orientation.

I believe it's important to pose these questions: Could vises be located at other workbench locations? Why not on the back corners or even the front center? Does a bench need a typical vise for the majority of woodworking functions? Are there manufactured and shop-made holding systems that could replace the standard vise? The answers are probably yes and no. First, it's very difficult to dismiss hundreds of years of workbench design. The modern vise is the evolutionary end-product of thousands upon thousands of hours spent at a workbench. The result of this research and development is that man is a clever creature, and innovations are always just a blink of an eye away. Look in any tool catalog, current or historic, and there are hundreds of clamping and holding devices. Quite possibly, a few might work better for your applications than a standard vise.

What you do want is the ability to firmly secure workpieces with a holding device that is quick and easy to operate. For example, the traditional vise with a long metal screw, approximately 1"×12", requires time and effort to turn the handle in order to open

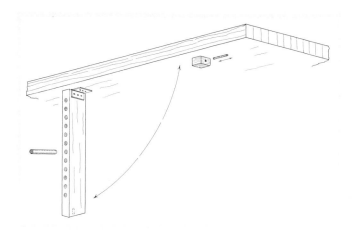

Support piece that is hinged to the underside of the workbench top. When not in use, the support piece is secured to the underside of the bench top via an attached block of wood that has a hole through it. A thin dowel is then inserted through the block and into the hole at the bottom of the support piece.

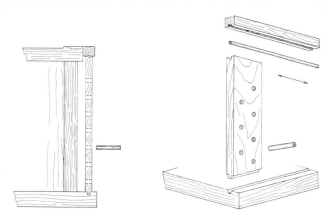

This drawing shows the details of movable support. Support top has a tenon and slides in a groove on the underside of the bench top. Support bottom has half-round groove (cove cut) and slides on a metal rod that is attached to a frame piece. Use metal dowels in support pieces because wooden dowels can be broken with heavy workpieces.

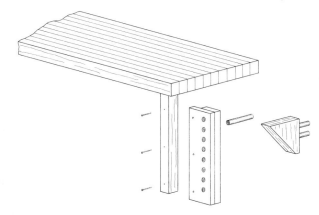

Simple support piece that attaches to workbench leg. Two types of workpiece holders are shown: single dowel and adjustable platform, which has two dowels for strength and rigidity.

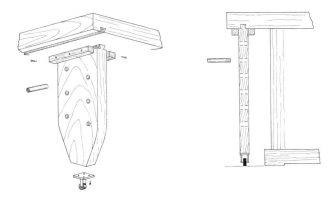

Another design of a support piece. It has reinforced dovetail fit to the underside of the workbench and a small roller (wheel) on the bottom. Extra braces at the top are necessary for minimizing "racking" motion.

or close the vise. The option is the manufactured vise with a quick-release trigger. If the vise is open to its widest point (approximately 14″) and you need to close it, simply squeeze the trigger and slide the vise face to the closed position. This requires minimum effort and much less time than a traditional vise. If you

feel that this comparison is unfair, I would suggest that you time yourself opening and closing both vise types ten times and see which you prefer.

If you choose to use metal vises, be sure to attach wooden faces to the jaws. Often these vises don't close together perfectly, so it's necessary to adjust

the wooden faces with shims until the jaws are parallel when closed. To maintain vises, periodically tighten the mounting bolts, keep the screw mechanism clean and free of debris, and once in a while add a dab of grease to the mechanism.

Another useful accessory is created by attaching a hinged leg to the underside of the bench. This leg (1″×3″× distance to floor) should have through-holes several inches apart into which a ½″ metal rod is positioned. The rod then acts as a support for long boards clamped in the front vise. When not in use, the leg is returned to the underside of the bench and secured with a pin.

Other vise-type options worth considering for the workbench include:

- leg vises
- patternmaker's vise
- machinist's vise
- miter vises
- wedges
- bench holdfasts
- bench hooks
- toggle clamps
- band clamps
- rope

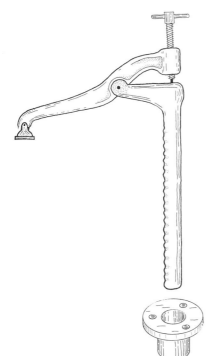
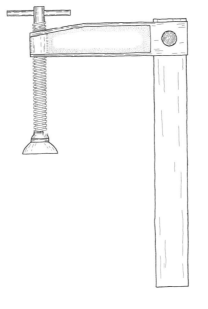
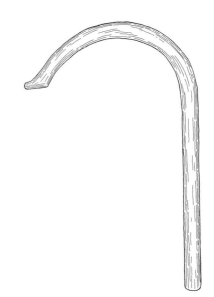

Three types of bench hold-downs; two are adjustable for increasing and releasing grip on workpiece. The third is fastened and released using a mallet.

10

BUILDING SAFETY INTO SHOP DESIGN

■

Safety is the factor that has extraordinary consequences in the present and the future.

Is your workshop a safe place? Just think about this: Some of the most dangerous objects and materials that you will ever come across are in the woodworking workshop. This includes just about everything that is used in the workshop: machines, hand tools, solvents, wood and sawdust. The physical activity of lifting or moving heavy objects, breathing solvent fumes, touching various chemicals, listening to high-decibel sounds, holding vibrating electrical tools and climbing on stepladders are some of the obstacles that need to be safely managed.

Woodworkers, especially those with home workshops, have had a long history of being unmonitored by the agencies that scrutinize commercial workshops. However, if you notice modern safety trends, there probably are (or will be) people and organizations who want to control what goes on in home workshops. While there has been a trickling down of valuable safety products to the home woodshop, I can't imagine that many people want to have sanctioning groups dictating home workshop procedures and necessities. Having said that, most woodworkers are doing a good job of learning how to do safe woodworking. Of course, there are many old, worn-out or poorly modified tools sold at garage sales or passed down through families. And these should be identified and gotten rid of so that accidents won't happen. How-

ever, in addition to operating machinery safely, we should also improve our handling of heavy materials (thus reducing body sprains and strains) and our use of chemicals (solvents and finishing products). After a fashion, the amateur woodworker and the one-person, small-business workshop want the best of two different worlds: the freedom of the hobby and craft world, and the tools, materials, techniques and business of the professional and commercial world. While this may seem fair if you are a home woodworker, the problem is that there are potentially unsafe workshop situations not being corrected.

The best advice that I can give you concerning safety is: Don't ignore it. The concept of safety is more important than your choice of table saw or favorite lumber. Besides, if you dismiss the importance of safety, it will become someone else's concern. It's reasonable to assume that we could one day see the advent of safety inspectors for the home workshop.

It is up to each of us to be individually responsible for having safe workshops. Please don't *pretend* that your workshop is safe or that it's too expensive to do the right thing, or don't come up with some other rationalization that keeps you from upgrading questionable situations. Make your workshop safe, learn proper woodworking techniques and never attempt to use tools or supplies in unsafe ways. Stay current on new tools, accessories and supplies. For example, router bits are now available in bright colors that are visible when the router is operating. Manufacturers often improve their products to comply with new safety guidelines. A few manufacturers actually make their products safer because of consumer demands. Remember, there are righteous people gathering statistical data on injuries so that they have the political strength to affect what you and I enjoy most—woodworking.

The initial steps toward workshop safety begin with the idea that you have to be aware of your surroundings.

■ Always look for the accident that's about to happen.
■ Don't ignore potential accidents or dangerous conditions.
■ Always evaluate the situation and ask yourself, "Is this the best way of doing something or is there a safer way?"
■ If there's a potential safety problem, take the appropriate steps to correct it.
■ Periodically review all workshop safety considerations.

SAFETY CHECKLIST

This list is not definitive. It is meant as a basic overview and a starting point for your own quest for a safe workshop.

General Safety Concerns
❑ Never work when you are tired.
❑ Never work or use tools and machinery when under the influence of alcohol, drugs or medications.
❑ Wear suitable work clothing that is not loose fitting or with dangling sleeves, ties, etc.
❑ Remove all jewelry, ties and scarfs, and tie up long hair.
❑ Wear safety goggles or glasses that have side guards.
❑ Wear hearing protection when operating machinery and power tools.
❑ Have approved and fully charged fire extinguishers in the workshop.
❑ Don't wear gloves while opera-

ting tools and machinery.
❑ Keep up-to-date insurance information on yourself, others using the workshop and the workshop itself. Check with your insurance company on policy coverage relating to accidents and other woodshop misfortunes.
❑ Keep a list of emergency telephone numbers near the telephone.
❑ Know where to go for emergency medical treatment.
❑ Stay current on codes, laws and other regulations pertaining to safety and hazardous materials, equipment and procedures.

Safety Preparation and Maintenance
❑ Read, understand and follow all instructions in the owner's manual for all machines and tools.
❑ Keep all owner's manuals in a handy location.
❑ Maintain all machines and tools to the manufacturer's recommendations.
❑ Use machine safety guards provided by the manufacturer.
❑ Don't modify safety guards or other safety-related equipment.
❑ Be sure that any modification to a tool or machine is either approved by the manufacturer or within the design limits of the tool.
❑ Before adding any accessory

to a tool or machine, be sure that it is both acceptable and safe.

❏ Use tools and machines for their intended purposes.

❏ Periodically review owner's manuals for safe operating procedures.

❏ Periodically inspect cutting tools, such as tungsten-carbide table saw blades and router bits, for damage or cracks. Replace as necessary.

❏ Keep cutting tools sharp.

Work Area Safety

❏ Do not work with a cluttered floor or with unstable piles of tools and materials.

❏ Wheels on mobile bases must be secured before using the machine.

❏ Prevent unauthorized use of the woodshop by installing lockable on/off switches on all machines.

❏ Have proper lighting and ventilation.

❏ Read and follow label information, including all warnings and cautions, prior to using solvents, finishing products or other chemicals, and follow all recommended use and safety procedures. If you have any concerns about products, call the manufacturer, your own physician, health agencies or the EPA.

❏ Not all rubber gloves are the same. Use the correct type

when working with solvents, finishing products, paint strippers, etc.

❏ Never dispose of oily rags in sealed trash cans that will be exposed to heat or direct sunlight.

❏ Store solvents and other flammable materials in approved storage units.

❏ Never use flammable solvents or other flammable finishing products near water heaters or any other high-temperature device or open flame.

Equipment Safety

❏ Use vises, clamps or other safe holding devices to firmly hold work material.

❏ If you are considering buying used equipment, be very cautious about missing parts, modifications, wobbly shafts and belts, and any other loose, damaged, bent or out-of-the-norm condition. When possible, ask for owner's manual and parts list.

❏ Don't buy used air compressors. The problem is that you can't see rust and corrosion inside the air tank.

❏ Absolutely never even consider buying an air compressor that has patched pinholes in the air tank.

Electrical Safety

❏ Comply with local electrical codes concerning wiring type,

conduits, hookups, service panels and other electrical features.

❏ Have the correct amperage and type fuses or circuit breakers installed in the electrical service.

❏ Light fixtures should have bulbs with the correct wattage.

❏ Halogen-type lights generate considerable heat and should be kept away from accidental bumping and flammable materials.

❏ Electrical motors, power tools and machines should have their technical information plates attached.

❏ Electrical motors, power tools and machines should have labels indicating that the product has been tested by a nationally recognized testing laboratory.

❏ Replace frayed or worn electrical cords.

❏ Replace electrical cords that have worn or bent plugs.

❏ Replace electrical cords nicked by sharp tools.

❏ There should be no standing water or moisture where electrical devices are used.

❏ Don't use unnecessary or overloaded extension cords.

❏ If extension cords are used, be sure to use correct wire gauge.

❏ Don't use modified adapter plugs: All three prongs should be intact.

❏ Don't use adapters that have a missing ground prong or a

missing grounding wire.

❑ Electrical cords shouldn't be placed in walkways or traffic areas.

❑ Don't have heavy objects resting on electrical cords.

❑ Electrical cords should be well away from spinning or operating machinery.

❑ Unplug electrical cords when adjusting or performing maintenance on machines and power tools.

❑ Electrical cords shouldn't be fastened down with nails or staples.

❑ The workshop should have a sufficient number of well-placed electrical receptacles.

❑ All outlets must work properly.

❑ Unused outlets should have safety covers placed in receptacle openings.

❑ GFI (ground fault circuit interrupters) outlets should be installed near sinks or other wet areas.

❑ Never use sparking electrical motors or tools near dust, oily rags or solvent fumes.

❑ Ventilation fans must be non-sparking and certified for ventilation of flammable fumes.

❑ There should be air circulation around electrical tools.

❑ Portable heaters must be listed as having been tested and approved for use in woodworking environments.

❑ Never use portable heaters near flammable materials such as rags, dust, scrap wood, finishing supplies, paper and drapes.

❑ Position approved portable heaters so that they can't be tipped over.

❑ Check for unnecessary machinery vibrations that can cause wear or stress on electrical wiring.

❑ Never leave woodburning tools, soldering irons, hot-glue guns, heat guns or other high-temperature tools unattended, and unplug these tools immediately after using them.

HEATING THE WORKSHOP

Heating the workshop often seems like both a necessity and a luxury. When the weather is poor, there's a natural desire to stay indoors and work in the shop. Additionally, heating will maintain the workshop at a constant temperature and humidity level, and hence stabilize wood and reduce rust and mildew.

The fundamental question: Is it safe to have heating within the workshop? After all, wood, sawdust, dust and finishing products are all potentially dangerous and flammable materials.

The common heating choices are:

■ *Central heating.* Route a new duct from the central heating system to the workshop.

■ *Central heating furnace in-stalled within workshop.* This seems like a workable concept as long as flammable solvents and materials are not used near the furnace.

■ *Baseboard heaters.* I've heard many discussions about this solution, but I haven't seen many workshops that have the room for anything at baseboard locations.

■ *Woodburning stoves.* It seems like a logical idea—scrap wood and a woodburning stove—but the idea of flames and hot metal surfaces in the same room as dust and lacquer or paint thinner seems too risky.

■ *Portable or space heaters.* Have you ever counted how many news stories there are every winter about fires started by portable and space heater mishaps?

■ *Radiant floor heating.* There are no hot spots or open flames, but the heating coils or hoses have to be installed in a new construction.

Check with your local safety and fire departments about what is safe and permitted in your area. If you have purchased a furnace, stove, portable heater or some other type of retrofitted heating system, call the manufacturer and ask about the safety of the product when it's used in a woodworking workshop.

Resources

This list is not meant to be encyclopedic. Rather than list every possible woodworking resource, I'm listing those that I have read, used, enjoyed and feel comfortable about recommending.

MAGAZINES

Fine Woodworking by Taunton Press,
63 S. Main St., P.O. Box 5507, Newtown, CT 06470
(800) 283-7252
http://www.taunton.com
E-mail: fw@Taunton.com

Wood from Better Homes and Gardens
1716 Locust Street, Des Moines, IA 50309-3023
(800) 374-9663
http://woodmagazine.com
E-mail: woodmail@woodmagazine.com

Woodshop News
35 Pratt Street, Essex, CT 06426
(860) 767-8227
http://www.woodshopnews.com
E-mail: woodshop@ix.netcom.com

Woodsmith
2200 Grand Avenue, Des Moines, IA, 50312
(515) 282-7000
http://www.augusthome.cpm
E-mail: Woodsmith@woodsmith.com

BOOKS

How-To and Technical Information

Build Your Own Mobile Power Tool Centers, John McPherson, Betterway Books, 1995

Dictionary of Woodworking Tools, R.A. Salaman, Taunton Press, 1975

Make Your Own Jigs & Workshop Furniture, Jeff Greef, Betterway Books, 1994

Tage Frid Teaches Woodworking, Tage Frid, Volumes 1,2,3, Taunton Press, 1979, 1981, 1985

Setting Up Your Own Woodworking Shop, Bill Stankus, Sterling, 1993

Tune Up Your Tools, Sal Maccarone, Betterway Books, 1996

Understanding Wood, R. Bruce Hoadley, Taunton Press, 1980

Understanding Wood Finishing, Bob Flexner, Rodale Press, 1994

Wood Joiner's Handbook, Sam Allen, Sterling, 1990

Woodworking With the Router, Bill Hylton and Fred Matlack, Rodale Press, 1993

Inspirational and Design

Japanese Woodworking Tools: Their Tradition, Spirit and Use, Toshio Odate, Taunton Press, 1984

The Fine Art of Cabinetmaking, James Krenov, Van Nostrand Reinhold, 1975

The Furniture of Gustav Stickley, Joseph J. Bavaro and Thomas L. Mossman, Van Nostrand Reinhold, 1982

The Nature and Aesthetics of Design, David Pye, Van Nostrand Reinhold, 1978

Sam Maloof, Woodworker, Sam Maloof, Kodansha International Ltd., 1983

Books by Eric Sloane (Ballantine Publishing—these are hard to find and mostly out of print, but worth searching for):

ABC Book of Early Americana

A Museum of Early American Tools

A Reverence for Wood

An Age of Barns

Diary of an Early American Boy

Eric Sloane's America

TOOL AND SUPPLY CATALOGS

Air Handling Systems, Manufacturer's Service Co.
(dust collector ductwork and fittings)
5 Lunar Drive, Woodbridge, CT 06525
(800) 367-3828
http://www.airhand.com
E-mail: jscott@airhand.com

Forrest Manufacturing Co., Inc.
(tungsten-carbide saw blades)
457 River Road, Clifton, NJ 07014
(800) 733-7111

Garrett Wade Co.
(general hand tools and supplies, some power tools)
161 Avenue of the Americas, New York, NY 10013
(800) 221-2942
http://www.garrettwade.com
E-mail: mail@garrettwade.com

HTC Products, Inc.
(mobile bases)
P.O. Box 839, Royal Oak, MI 48068-0839
(800) 624-2027

The Japan Woodworker
(traditional Japanese hand tools, some general tools)
1731 Clement Avenue, Alameda, CA 94501
(800) 537-7820
http://www.japanwoodworker.com
E-mail: fdamsen@ix.netcom.com

Klingspor's Sanding Catalogue
P.O. Box 3737, Hickory, NC 28603-3737
(800) 228-0000
http://www.sandingcatalog.com

Oneida Air Systems, Inc.
(cyclone dust collectors, fittings, filter bags)
1005 W. Fayette Street, Syracuse, NY 13204
(315) 476-5151
http://www.dreamscape.com/oasinc
E-mail: oasinc@dreamscape.com

Packard Woodworks
(lathe turning supplies)
P.O. Box 718, 101 Miller Road, Tryon, NC 28782
(800) 683-7876

Seven Corners Ace Hardware
(discount mail order, mostly power tools)
216 West 7th Street, St. Paul, MN 55102
(800) 328-0457
http://www.7cornershdwe.com

Tool Crib of the North
(discount mail order, mostly power tools)
P.O. Box 14040, Grand Forks, ND 58208-4040
(800) 358-3096
http://www.toolcribofthenorth.com

Wilke Machinery Co.
(machinery for home and commercial workshops)
3230 Susquehanna Trail, York, PA 17402-9716
(717) 764 5000

The Woodturner's Catalog
(lathe turning supplies)
1287 E. 1120 S., Provo, UT 84606
(800) 551 8876
http://www.craftusa.com

Wood Carvers Supply, Inc.
(carving tools and supplies)
P.O. Box 7500, Englewood, FL 34295-7500
(941) 698-0123

The Woodworker's Store
(general supplies, some tools)
4365 Willow Drive, Medina, MN 55340
(800) 279-4441
http://www.woodworkerstore.com

Woodworker's Supply
(power tools, machinery, accessories, general supplies)
1108 North Glenn Road, Casper, WY 82601
(800) 645-9292

Woodcraft
(general hand tools and supplies, some power tools)
210 Wood County Industrial Park, P.O. Box 1686, Parkersburg, WV 26102
(800) 535-4482
http://www.woodcraft.com

INTERESTING ORGANIZATIONS

American Association of Woodturners (AAW)
3200 Lexington Avenue
Shoreview, MN 55126

Early American Industries Association
c/o Elton Hall, Executive Director
167 Bakerville
South Dartmouth, MA 02748-4198

The Furniture Society
P.O. Box 18
Free Union, VA 22940

Guild of American Luthiers
8222 South Park Avenue
Tacoma, WA 98408

Hardwood Manufacturer's Association
400 Penn Center Boulevard, Suite 530
Pittsburgh, PA 15235

International Wood Collector's Society (IWCS)
2300 W. Range Line Road
Greencastle, IN 46135

Mid-West Tool Collector's Association (M-WTCA)
Route 2, Box 152
Wartrace, TN 37183-9802

National Woodcarver's Association
P.O. Box 43218
Cincinnati, OH 45243

INDEX